DRIVING

IN THE HIMALAYAS

Sikkim

"Two roads diverged in a wood, and I —
I took the one less travelled by,
And that has made all the difference".

— ROBERT FROST

Author
Koko Singh
Editor
Annu Sharma
Photo Editor
Ipshita Barua
Photographs
Ipshita Barua
Annu Sharma
Koko Singh
Design
Pranab Dutta

Rupa & Co

Second Edition 2007

Rupa & Co

7/16, Ansari Road, Daryaganj,
New Delhi 110 002

Sales Centres:

Allahabad	Bangalore	Chandigarh
Chennai	Hyderabad	Jaipur
Kathmandu	Kolkata	Mumbai
Pune		

ACKNOWLEDGEMENTS

This book would not have been possible
without the assistance and guidance
received from Mr. R.B. Subba, the Minister
of Tourism, Govt. of Sikkim, as also
Mr. P.K. Dong. We would like to thank
Ms. Siphora Targain for poring over the
manuscript and Jigme Gyaltsen for looking
after us in Sikkim. All this could not have
been achieved without the help of Mr. G.P.
Upadhyay who showed extraordinary
interest and initiative when the project was
in its infancy.

Our journey would not have been
possible without the help rendered by Rajiv
and Malini Puri, specially since we trashed
their car! Thanks also to Tara Bedi whose
nimble fingers helped generate the
prototype on Marieke's antiquated laptop.

Printed in India by
Ajanta Offset & Packaging
New Delhi

Design and pre-press:
Great Latitude, New Delhi, India
www.greatlatitude.com

Cover: Mt. Kanchendzonga

CONTENTS

Terraced fields with a golden harvest of rice

DRIVING Holidays in the Himalayas is a series of books that endeavour to give the reader a glimpse of many exciting, exotic locales that can be easily accessed by road and hopes to provide enough insight to make your trip a comfortable and memorable one.

Whereas this book explores Sikkim, and briefly the adjoining towns of Darjeeling and Kalimpong, others in the series take you through Uttaranchal, Himachal, Ladakh & Zanskar.

These books especially focus on travellers who are fond of driving, have their own wheels (two, four – or even hired will do!), and love the mountains. Given the time constraints of our lives today, each book is designed to cover a fair degree of terrain in a week to ten days. Although it does not aim to visit every place possible in a region, it certainly traverses a reasonable cross-section. It reflects the author's own preferences of picturesque places to visit and also makes dining recommendations ▪

THE HIMALAYAS

THROUGH the ages, the Himalayas have been revered by millions of Indians as the abode of the Gods. The early 'rishis' (sages), referred to them as "the expanse of the two arms of the Supreme Being", suggestive of the whole world being locked in the Himalaya's divine embrace.

Writing in the fifth century AD, Kalidas, the renowned poet, has an evocative but apt description—

In the northern quarter is divine Himalayas,
  the lord of the Mountains,
  reaching from Eastern to Western Ocean,
  firm as a rod to measure the earth......
  There demigods rest in the shade of clouds,
  which spread like a girdle below the peaks but when the rains disturb them,
    they fly to sunlit summits.......

It is here that Shiva, the great god of destruction, found solace after the death of his consort, Sati, and atoned for almost destroying the world with his dance, the 'Tandava Nritya'. After wooing the bereaved Shiva for over a thousand years, Parvati, the daughter of the mountains succeeded in winning his love. The Himalayas are studded with temples dedicated to Shiva and

Machapuchre or 'Fish Tail'
viewed from Pokhra, Nepal

Parvati, and every year devotees in untold numbers travel hundreds, if not thousands, of kilometers, to visit their 'abode'.

In the words of the *Skanda Purana*: "As the sun dries the morning dew, so are the sins of man dissipated at the sight of the Himalaya".

Centuries of pilgrimage led to the building of numerous temples and hermitages, but not a single 'hill station', as we know it.

In earlier times, the local inhabitants were unaffected as the transient pilgrims were extremely limited in number due to the difficulties and time required for the arduous journey.

The first planned hill retreats were set up by the great Mughal emperors Akbar, Shah Jehan, and Jehangir who established summer palaces around Srinagar in the state of Jammu & Kashmir. The beautiful Nishat and Shalimar gardens are testament to those early endeavours and are a star attraction even today. The Mughals faded into oblivion and were followed by the British, a unique creature, unlike any other who ruled the subcontinent. They made little effort to absorb or integrate with the ancient cultures and traditions they found in this land. They were masters at the game of intrigue and treachery, playing one powerful local ruler against the other to extend and consolidate their

grip over the country. However, one enemy continued to challenge – the climate.

One of the main problems faced by the British was keeping the army of almost 100,000 troops healthy. Soldiers garrisoned in the hill forts were found to be much better off than their comrades in the plains and this started the search for resorts to be used as sanatoriums.

In 1819, the first 'hill station' was established at Shimla (now the capital of Himachal Pradesh) and over the next seventy years, around eighty hill stations were developed all over the country. Situated on hill tops and often even in places without a local populace, the Raj used the ample resources at its command to construct roads and railways under the most challenging conditions – who else could build railway lines to remote Darjeeling and Shimla! To give them due kudos, it is thanks to their eccentricities and desire to create conditions akin to those 'back home', far from the enervating heat, that such an extensive network of roads developed, allowing us our much-coveted driving holidays in the Himalayas.

Geologically speaking, the Himalayas are the youngest mountain range in the world and are actually still growing – up to 0.8cm annually. Samples extracted from the slopes of Mt. Everest confirm that in the past millennia, what is today the world's highest and longest (East to West) mountain range was once part of a vast ocean bed!

Eighty million years ago, in the period when dinosaurs roamed the earth – the Jurassic Age – the earth's land mass split into two great continents, Laurasia in the northern hemisphere and Gondwanaland in the southern hemisphere. Later the land mass, that is the Indian subcontinent, broke away from Gondwanaland and floated across the Earth's surface till it ran into Asia! The collision between the hard volcanic rock of India and Asia's soft sedimentary crust resulted in the creation of all the Asian mountain ranges such as the Karakoram, Hindu Kush, Pamir, as also the Tien Shan and Kun Lun. This process took between five and seven million years and the fact that the Himalayas are at the front of the continental collision accounts for their dwarfing the other ranges and for their

Bar headed geese over the Tso Moriri Lake in Ladakh

The Himalayas stretch 2500km from Nanga Parbat in the West (in Pakistan), to Namche Barwa (Arunachal Pradesh), in the East. The range boasts of fourteen peaks in excess of 26,200ft/8000m, including Mt. Everest which at 29,028ft/8848m is the highest mountain in the world. The highest peak in our country is the third highest in the world – mighty Kanchendzonga, 28,160ft/8585m, located in the second smallest state, Sikkim.

The Himalayan range is actually three almost parallel mountain systems. At the top lies the Great Himalayan Range with perennial snow peaks rising to heights in excess of 16,500ft/5000m, preceded by the Middle Himalayan Range of peaks averaging between 13,000-16,500ft/4000-5000m. The foothills, or the Lower Himalayan Range, are the ranges bordering the plains with mountains upto 8000ft/2500m in height and, regrettably, it is only in this third, and lowest, layer of mountains that most of our driving journeys are confined!

The Himalayas are also the source of the three major river systems of the subcontinent – the Indus, the Ganga, and the Brahmaputra. All these originate from glaciers, one of which, Gaumukh – the source of the holy Ganga – is only a few kilometers from the road-head at Gangotri in Uttarakhand

Kumaoni slate roofed houses with 'Likhai' woodwork

S IKKIM is the second smallest state of our country measuring a mere 65km East to West and 110km North to South. This 7096 sq km accounts for only 0.22% of the total area of our country but encompasses an astounding range of pristine natural beauty. From one of

The Changay waterfall near Pelling, W. Sikkim

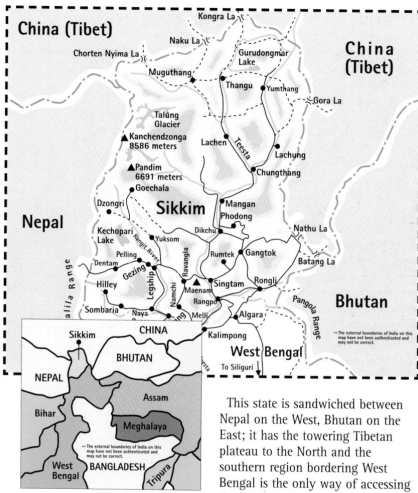

This state is sandwiched between Nepal on the West, Bhutan on the East; it has the towering Tibetan plateau to the North and the southern region bordering West Bengal is the only way of accessing the area.

Almost two-thirds of the state is mountainous – with ten peaks in excess of 20,000ft/6000m on the western border, and six massifs of similar stature on the eastern border. The Tibetan plateau marks the northern border, the Chola &

the highest mountain peaks in the world, the towering Kanchendzonga, to virgin tropical forests; from alpine meadows and rhododendron forests to rushing streams, rivers and incredible waterfalls – Sikkim has it all and more!

Pangolia ranges lie to the East and the Singelila range on the western side. The mighty Teesta River originates in the far North from a glacier above Cholamu Lake. The nearby Gurudongmar Lake is an additional source for the Teesta. The river starts as a tiny trickle of almost frozen water from an altitude of over 17,000ft/5150m, but turns into a torrential, awesome river within a very short distance of under 100km. Along with the Rangit, which starts from the central mountain range, these two rivers form the southern frontier with West Bengal. Another spur of the Himalayas, that originates from the Tibetan plateau, separates the Lachen and Lachung valleys which are, in my perception, one of the most beautiful and spectacular regions of Sikkim. The area, ringed in by a horseshoe of mountains, descends steeply from lofty heights of 18,000ft/5500m in the northern plateau to 2000ft/600m in a span of only 80km.

As per the 2001 census the total population of the state is just under 550,000, which is a mere 0.05% of our country's population! Gangtok, the capital, accounts for around ten percent people and the state is represented by one member each in the Lok and Rajya Sabha. The local assembly has thirty two members and literacy is a highly respectable seventy percent ■

Views of mountain ranges on the drive up

GETTING THERE

ONE would imagine that this would be a difficult, time-consuming exercise but the exact opposite is true!

There are daily morning flights to Bagdogra (near Siliguri) in West Bengal. From here to Gangtok, the capital and the starting point of your holiday, is just a very pleasant three to four hour drive by road. So you could actually start from Mumbai, Delhi or Chennai in the morning and be in Gangtok by late afternoon! Return flights are also conveniently scheduled in the afternoon. So getting back home — wherever that is — in a matter of hours, is very possible.

For those who do not like flying, overnight train connections to New Jalpaiguri (30km from Siliguri), like

Travelling from
the airport on the
Pankhabari road

the Guwahati bound Rajdhani from New Delhi and several others from Kolkata, are a convenient option.

From Siliguri, or New Jalpaiguri, to Gangtok the principal connection is by road – a 125km journey from either the airport or the railway station. The road routes through dense forest just outside Siliguri and ascends as a surprisingly good mountain road, large sections of which run along the beautiful but frisky Teesta River. There are numerous picturesque spots along the way for a 'chai-break'. At a few places such as Kalijhora, (5km after the Coronation Bridge), or the confluence of the Relli and Teesta, (approximately another 15km ahead), you can climb down to the river and have a picnic lunch washed down with a beverage of your choice.

The journey takes between three to four hours and your travel operator can arrange a jeep, Maruti van, Qualis or the good old Ambassador, depending on your preference. (Luxury buses are available from Siliguri to Gangtok and take around five hours for the trip).

There is also a helicopter service from Bagdogra to Gangtok, which the company Pawan Hans operates on a regular basis, subject of course, to weather conditions.

Foreign nationals require an inner line permit to visit Sikkim (refer page 175) ■

TRAVEL WITHIN THE REGION

Private vehicles are discouraged in N. Sikkim and some parts of E. Sikkim. Travel in these regions can be organised by your tour operator who takes care of accommodation, meals, transportation and a guide (optional), as also permits wherever required. Your own vehicle would be useful in Gangtok and in W. Sikkim.

PETROL PUMPS

There are not very many petrol pumps other than on the main highway to Gangtok.
Since you will probably not take your own vehicle to N. Sikkim, make sure your tour operator's vehicle is adequately stocked. There is a petrol pump at Gyalsing (Geysing) in W. Sikkim which takes care of your needs in that region. Remember, distances are short and a full tank will cover you from Gangtok to Pelling and around. Topping up at Gyalsing will see you back to Siliguri via Darjeeling though of course, both Darjeeling and Kalimpong also have petrol pumps. Repair shops are few and far between, but are available all along the main highway to Gangtok (at Singtam, Rangpo, Melli, Ranipul) and also at towns like Jorethang, Namche, Pelling, Gyalsing, Ravangla, Legship.

Corn being dried before the onset of winter

SIKKIM, despite its small size, enjoys virtually all climate conditions, barring the blistering heat of the plains! It is possible to be walking in snow even in summer and descend to a tropical forest in the span of two to three hours!

Maximum temperatures in the summer months are around 35°C in the areas adjoining W. Bengal but the temperature for the most of your holiday will not exceed 25°C, whereas in some areas the minimum can be close to 0°C. Sikkim experiences a very heavy monsoon and Gangtok receives over 350cm of rain in the year! Delhi at 61cm is a poor cousin in this respect, and even Mumbai at 230cm pales in comparison! Cherrapunji, considered the wettest place in India, gets 1100cm rainfall in the year.

Due to its close proximity to the Bay of Bengal, even a small depression over it can trigger a downpour in Sikkim. Hence, even in the spring (April-May), rainfall is quite common, particularly in the afternoon when the mercury has risen. It is only between October and March that the weather is uniformly clear with minimal rainfall. Keeping weather conditions in mind, we recommend March 1st – May 15th and October 1st – December 15th as the best time to visit Sikkim.

Spring, the former period of these two, is preferable as it coincides with the flowering season (April 1st – May 15th) of rhododendrons in the Lachung valley as well as Varsey. The annual Orchid Festival in Gangtok is also held at this time. During the October-December period there is virtually no haze to 'cloud' the view and you can see the majestic snow peaks shimmer against a startling blue sky. The clear views continue till March end but December to February can be very cold.

Those looking for peace and quiet to commune with nature should time their trip just before or after the peak tourist season. The only time to really avoid visiting Sikkim is mid-May to September end as it gets very wet. A word of caution here – it is important to track the progress of the monsoon as it may catch you unawares earlier in May in some years and that could be a real dampener, literally!!

Despite the time you visit, warm clothes need to be carried as the evenings can be chilly, and you will be spending some nights at altitudes around 9000ft/2750m during your trip. Some day journeys also involve travel to places at altitudes above 12,000ft/3650m, and what may seem to be a warm day at your starting point, may turn frigid in a matter of a couple of hours ■

A storm gathering over Menmecho Lake, not far from Gangtok

FLORA AND FAUNA

FLORA

Sikkim is host to an amazing array of verdant oak and bamboo forests. Since the climate is a combination of tropical, temperate and alpine, the variation and diversity you can experience in a single day cannot fail to stun the senses. It is no wonder that Sikkim is touted as the one place where such a brilliant

Wild tree-orchids by the roadside

state flower. There are also thirty species of rhododendrons, found mainly in places above 10,000ft/3000m. This is the state tree and it comes in hues of yellow, red, pink, purple and mauve.

The crops grown are mainly millet, maize and rice, but unknown to most, Sikkim is the capital of *badi elaichi* (black cardamom), which is found in abundance around Mangan, the headquarters of the northern district and on your route to the Lachen/ Lachung valleys. Sikkim tea, grown at government estates at Temi, is known for its unique flavour.

FAUNA

Yaks belong to the cattle family but thrive at altitudes of 10,000ft/3000m and more. They have been domesticated in Sikkim and are used for carrying loads and for their thick milk that is converted into a hardened cheese called 'churpi'. Their meat is also eaten and the hide and hair is used for making circular tents called yurts. The yak has been crossed with the cow and this species, the 'Dzo', survives at lower altitudes.

The red panda, from the raccoon family, is the state animal and is found at altitudes between 7000 and 10,000ft/2125-3000m. It lives

array of natural diversity can be found in such a compact area. The region is particularly renowned for its variety of 600 species of orchids – of which the 'Noble Orchid' is the

on tree tops, close to forests of bamboo, whose leaves are its staple diet.

Other animals that inhabit the snow bound region of the North are the Tibetan wild ass (kiang), the bharal (blue sheep) and the tahir-like goat, the shapi.

With some measure of luck, these can be spotted in the wild in the Fambhong Lho Wildlife Sanctuary 20km outside Gangtok, but can certainly be seen in the Himalayan Zoological Park in Gangtok.

An incredibly large kaleidoscopic variety of butterflies – around 500 species – are to be found in Sikkim, adding not just colour but vibrancy to the idyllic atmosphere of the forests.

For bird lovers, this is a paradise! Close to half the entire subcontinent's birdlife, approximately 550 species make this tiny state their habitat — ranging from the little 9cm long olive ground warbler to the huge bearded eagle whose wingspan is 2.5m! The noted ornithologist, Dr. Salim Ali, in his book *Birds of Sikkim*, has covered this amazing concentration of birdlife extensively. Another good reference book is *A Birdwatchers Guide to India* by Krys Kazmierczak and Raj Singh ∎

The elusive snow leopard in the Darjeeling zoo

If you are an avid birdwatcher, a 'bird watching safari' in the Doars area of W. Bengal comes highly recommended by those who have been there. The Gorumara National Park and adjacent Chapramari Wildlife Sanctuary are only 75km away from Siliguri. The Lava, Nera and Rushet forests around Kalimpong are also a favourite. Within Sikkim, the best spotting is around Ravangla in the Maenem Sanctuary as also the nearby Fambhong Lho Wildlife Sanctuary. Several other species are found around Pemayangtse, Sangochoeling and Kechopari Lake.

HISTORY

THE Lepchas (ravine folk), are believed to be the original settlers of Sikkim, arriving here sometime in the thirteenth century. Originating from Assam and Bhutan, they are of Mongoloid descent and were tribals who followed the Bon faith and whose deities were the spirits of the mountains, rivers and forests. They have their own script and language and their songs and legends are testament to their strong bonds with their rugged natural environment.

Sometime in the fourteenth century the Bhutias, (which is the Nepalese word for the people of 'Bhot', as Tibet was called), migrated to Sikkim from Tibet and established the Sakya kingdom. Guru Tashi, a prince from Tibet, was inspired by a divine vision to migrate here and his family helped the reigning Sakya king in the construction of a monastery. His son, Khye Bumsa, is said to have raised the pillars of this monastery single handed.

Khye Bumsa married the Sakya king's daughter and established contact with the Lepcha chieftain, Thekong Tek, in Gangtok. Subsequently, a treaty of brotherhood was signed between the two at Kabi Longstok. As time went on, the Lepchas broke into small clans and ultimately came under the protection of Khye Bumsa's grandson Phunstok, born in 1604.

Around this time events in Tibet compelled the followers of the Red Hat sect (Nyingma) to flee to Bhutan and Sikkim to escape persecution. Among them was the Lama Lhatsun Chembo who came with the divine mission of establishing a Buddhist monastery in Sikkim. Later he was joined by two others, Sempa Chembo and Rinzing Chembo, at Norbugang, (modern day Yuksom, 'the meeting place of three superior beings'). They established contact with Phunstok,

the Sakya king, who travelled to Yuksom with his family and followers and became the first king – or Chogyal ('righteous ruler') – of Sikkim in 1642, taking on the surname 'Namgyal'. Under his regime the borders of Sikkim were expanded to include the Chumbi valley in Tibet, Darjeeling, Kalimpong and a part of modern day Nepal and Bhutan. The capital was established in Yuksom and the name Sikkim became common parlance being

derived from the word 'Su Khim' meaning 'New House'. Around 1670, his son shifted the capital to Rabdentse, near the Pemayangtse Monastery and Pelling. A family schism in the next generation led to one faction inviting the Bhutanese army who took Rabdentse as also Kalimpong. The monarchy was subsequently restored but in the reign of Tenzing Namgyal (1780-93),

Rabdentse Palace ruins near Pelling

Tashiding Gompa in W. Sikkim

the Nepali king invaded and drove him out of Rabdentse into Tibet. Being over ambitious, the Nepalese ventured into Tibet too and this led to a Chinese counterattack and the defeat of the Nepalese. The Sino-Nepalese treaty restored the Sikkimese monarchy and the next king, realising that Rabdentse was too close to Nepal for comfort,

moved the capital to Tumlong, near Gangtok. The Chinese continued to consider Sikkim a vassal state.

The subsequent history is intertwined with the intrigues and power plays of the British East India Company and later the British Empire. Looking to establish trade links with Tibet, Sikkim was identified as the best route and the British offered support to the Sikkim king to ward off the continuing

Nepalese incursions into its territory. In 1814, war between the British and the Nepalese led to the defeat of the latter and the subsequent restoration of all its former territories to Sikkim in 1817 (Treaties of Sigauli and Titalia).

Some years later, the British started looking for 'hill stations' in the East after having successfully established a growing 'chain' of such places in the western Himalayas – Shimla,

Darjeeling town with Kanchendzonga looking over it

Mussoorie, Nainital, Dalhousie, Ranikhet etc. The first attempt at Cherrapunji, in Assam, was literally washed away! They then turned their attention to 'Dorje-Ling', or the 'place of the thunderbolt', which was a sparsely inhabited, thickly forested area on the extreme western side of Sikkim. Negotiations with the

Chogyal resulted in the 'gifting' of Darjeeling in 1835 in return for absolutely nothing, other than an annual allowance, since the corresponding 'gift' of land from the British was never delivered. The Chogyal was thus landed with a British enclave within his kingdom, which disrupted his flow of trade and encouraged an influx of

Canon used by Col. Younghusband in his expedition to Tibet — Planters Club, Darjeeling

Nepalese settlers in and around Darjeeling. In addition, since the boundary was loosely demarcated, there were instances of taxes being collected by the British, from Sikkimese villages!

In 1849, the superintendent of Darjeeling, Dr. Campbell, was detained by the Sikkimese for entering the kingdom unannounced and without permission. Predictably, the Empire promptly struck back and annexed virtually the whole state of Sikkim and also stopped the annual

payment of Rs. 6000 to the Chogyal.

The British started building roads to enhance trade with Tibet and this led to clashes in 1886. In 1889, Claude White was appointed the first political officer of Sikkim and he functioned as the de facto ruler. The then Chogyal, Thu Tob Namgyal, shifted the capital to Gangtok in 1894. Having seen the Tibetans being defeated in 1888, the Chinese agreed to recognise British India's direct control over the external and internal affairs of Sikkim. In 1905, a British India expedition to Lhasa, led by Col. Younghusband, secured exclusive trading rights for the British in Tibet.

During this period, despite several agreements to restore his sovereignty, the Chogyal was kept in and out of detention by the British. In 1905 the visiting Prince of Wales, (the future King George V), met and liked the Sikkimese crown prince and this led to a widening of his

Mani wall at Tashiding Gompa

sovereign powers during his brief reign in 1914. Then onwards, this independence was allowed to grow and in 1918, Sikkimese independence in all domestic affairs was restored. Tashi Namgyal initiated major reforms such as banning child labour, indentured service and gambling. During the World War II, Sikkimese forces fought alongside the British in Burma (now Myanmar) and when India became independent, Sikkim was granted protectorate status.

Tashi Namgyal died in 1963 and was succeeded by his son Palden Thondup Namgyal, the twelfth and last Chogyal of the 300-year old dynasty.

The last hereditary ruler, the

Chogyal, Palden Thondup Namgyal, came to the throne faced with a growing sentiment among the citizens of Sikkim that the country should join with the Indian Union. The Chogyal's mismanagement of the situation led to riots in 1970 which intensified and culminated in elections, said to be rigged by the Chogyal, in 1973. In 1975, a pro-union government came to power and requested associate status. The Chogyal refused to recognise the move and instead broke with his ministers and asked them to tender their resignations. They refused and on April 10th, they declared the Chogyal's administrative functions to have ended and asked for the union of Sikkim with India, pending a referendum which was held four days later. On April 14th, 1975 the referendum approved merging with India with a thumping majority of 93% and Sikkim became the twenty-second state of India.

However, for reasons best known to itself, the Peoples Republic of China continued to show Sikkim as an independent state in its official maps – a position that has just changed in March 2004.

In September 1974, the leader of the Sikkim Congress, Kazi Lhendup Dorje, became the first chief minister. He was followed by Nar Bahadur Bhandari, of the Sikkim Sangram Parishad, in 1979, who remained in power till early 1994. He was succeeded by Pawan Chamling, who has just been re-elected chief minister in May 2004 for the third consecutive term, and is on his way to becoming the longest serving chief minister of the state ■

Monastery in the Gangtok Palace complex

RELIGION

T HOSE of Nepalese origin comprise seventy-five percent of the population of Sikkim while the Lepchas and Bhutias are around eighteen percent and six percent respectively. Almost a third of the entire population follows the Buddhist faith and the balance is predominantly Hindu. The Sikkimese landscape, besides offering panoramic beauty, is a treasure trove of majestic, beautiful 'gompas' (monasteries) and pagodas, called 'stupas' or 'chortens', that dominate the region. Since this is India's only state where Buddhism holds sway so prominently, a brief account of Buddhism and its introduction to Sikkim via Tibet is being provided. At the outset, apologies to those of the faith for whom this would appear to be perfunctory and shallow, but hopefully will be of some value to other travellers, as it was to the author whose knowledge initially was quite superficial!

BUDDHISM

Since most of us are familiar with the life of Siddhartha Gautam through our study of Indian history, only a brief sketch of it is being given. He was born over 2000 years ago to the royal family of Lumbini, which is a part of present day Nepal. At the age of twenty-nine, he renounced his family and all trappings of his life as a prince.

After following a path of penance and sacrifice, he achieved Nirvana, or enlightenment, while meditating under a Bodhi (Peepul) tree for six years. Over the next forty-five years, his teachings and discourses

provided the foundation of Buddhism, which is strictly speaking, less a religion and more a philosophy with a code of morality. According to these beliefs, asceticism and renunciation of material life do not necessarily lead to enlightenment. This can only be achieved after recognising and accepting the Four Noble Truths: the core tenet of Buddhist philosophy. According to these Truths, all life is

Inside the Ralong Monastery

suffering arising from our sensual desires and the illusion that they are important. Suffering can only end when this realisation is fully accepted and this in turn can only be achieved by following the prescribed Eight Fold Path. This path is that of right thought, right speech, right action, right way of life, right effort, right awareness, right intention and right concentration. This path leads to the extinguishing of desires and eventually a state of Nirvana, having been through a process of rebirths where your action in each life determines the next life. This is 'karma' which is not simply fate but the path which leads you

through the cycle of birth and death till you finally escape from the world of suffering. All human beings have the potential and the power to follow the path.

After the death of Gautam Buddha, referred to as Maha Parinirvana, the first Great Council of Disciples was held by Mahakasyapa in the kingdom of Magadh to record, clarify and consolidate the teachings of Buddha. This council lead to the Theravada Teachings (doctrine of elders), which is focused primarily on meditation and concentration – the eighth of the Eight Fold Path. As a result, this doctrine centered on a monastic life in which almost all the time was spent in meditation.

Buddhism developed rapidly in India under the patronage of King Ashoka in the third century BC and as his empire was vast, so was the spread of Buddhism. His children Mahindra and Sanghamitra are said to have carried the word of Buddhism to Sri Lanka. Missions were sent forth to other lands as well to spread the teachings of Buddha.

However, by the first century AD, the limitations of Buddhism's appeal (based on the individual working to achieve Nirvana, 'prati moksha', through meditation and the exclusion of a normal family life), were evident. A schism developed within the ranks of the followers with the objective of re-formulating the teachings of Buddhism to include and accommodate people from all walks of life and not only those who had renounced family life and

The Buddhist tradition is passed on through generations — evening prayers at a monastery

become 'monks'. This 'new Buddhism' was called Mahayana Buddhism – the Greater Vehicle or literally, the Greater Ox Cart, since it would accommodate believers from all walks of life. Theravada, which was the mainstream Buddhism till now, was then, somewhat superciliously, referred to as Hinayana Buddhism – the Lesser Vehicle.

Mahayana Buddhism can be compared to the Protestant reformers of sixteenth century Europe, where there is no claim for the creation of a new religion but rather 'recovery' of its original form. The Mahayanists claim that their canon of scriptures represented 'the final, refined teachings of Buddha', which had hitherto been extended only to the most faithful followers. Regardless of the controversy over its origins, the Mahayana doctrine represents a significant departure in the philosophy with the objective of extending religious authority to a greater number of people, rather than a concentration in the hands of a few.

The most important changes were:
(i) The Theravada goal of attainment of Buddhahood was in practice intimidating and seemingly unachievable. Hence Mahayanists tried to make Buddhism a more esoteric religion by introducing two grades of attainment below the level of Buddhahood. One is the Pratyeka-Buddha, or one who has awakened to the truth but keeps it a secret and the other the Arhant-Buddha or 'worthy-one', who has realised the truth by learning it from others. The Arhant is the goal for all believers – he hears the truth, comes to realise it as truth and then passes into Nirvana.

(ii) Another major innovation was the idea of Boddhisattava (Being of Wisdom), who lived many lives before attaining Buddhahood. Before Buddha entered his final life as Siddhartha Gautam, he had spent many lives working towards Buddhahood. In these previous lives, he was a 'Buddha-in-waiting' or Boddhisattava, who performed incredible acts of compassion and generosity towards his fellow human beings. Boddhisattavas do not want to evolve into a state of Buddhahood till they have freed all humanity from its suffering. Mahayana Buddhism also went against the original belief that there would be only one Buddha and that no more would follow – their belief suggests that Buddha has prophesied the coming of the future Buddha – who should currently be passing through one of the many cycles of life as the 'Maitreya' or Future Buddha. There is also a possibility of more than one Maitreya – if you're on the right track it could be

A novice at Enchey
Monastery

Goddess Tara at the
Rumtek Monastery

someone you know, or even yourself!

(iii) Lastly, Mahayana Buddhism 'converted' Buddhism from a philosophy to a religion. Theravada Buddhism believes that Buddha was a historical person who after his death ceased to exist. The Mahayanists developed the doctrine of the Three Bodies or Trikaya. As per this, the Buddha was not a human being but a manifestation of a universal spiritual being which had three bodies:

– when on earth as Siddhartha Gautam, it was the Body of Magical Transformation, 'Nirmanakaya'.

– this form emanated from the Body of Bliss, 'Sambhogakaya'. Located in heaven, this is the ruling and governing god of the Universe. This Body of Bliss has many forms and the one ruling our world is Amitava who lives in 'Sukhavati', the Land of Pure Bliss, a paradise located in the Western heavens.

– the Body of Bliss in turn emanates from the Body of Essence, 'Dharmakaya', which is the underlying rule and principle of the

Rotating the prayer wheels for good luck

Universe. This is akin to a universal soul and Nirvana the transcendent journey to it. Today Mahayana Buddhism is prevalent in Tibet, Ladakh, Japan, China and Vietnam while Theravada Buddhism prevails

A monk at prayer in the Sangochoeling Gompa

in Burma (now Myanmar), Thailand, Cambodia and Sri Lanka.

BUDDHISM IN SIKKIM

Sikkim came under the Buddhist influence via Tibet and, supposedly, this was foretold by the chief protagonist of Nyingmapa Buddhism, Guru Padmasambhava

(Rinpoche), when he travelled through Sikkim en route to Tibet in the eighth century AD. He was also one of the pioneers of Tantric or Mystic Buddhism, which evolved from Mahayana Buddhism, and encompasses the Vajrayana teachings. Tantric Buddhism is more esoteric and complex in nature and

Wearing shorts while visiting a gompa is not advisable and shoes should be removed before entering a prayer hall. The 'right' way of circumventing a chorten or gompa is from left to right i.e. in a clockwise direction. Monks who act as your guides do not expect any remuneration but contributions can be left in a donation box, provided for the purpose.

Monasteries have rules regarding photography and in the interest of preserving these irreplaceable works of art, it is important to follow the regulations and refrain from touching the frescoes and other religious objects on display. The visitor is expected to respect and maintain the sanctity and tranquillity of the environment.

is found in Ladakh and Sikkim, having originated in Tibet. The Supreme Tantra combines male and female tantras, one of which is the deity Kalchakra. Meditation and rituals conducted towards this deity, and his consort Viswamata, for attaining Nirvana are known as the Kalchakra Puja. The Dalai Lama is the ultimate authority in teaching this puja, which His Holiness performs to initiate disciples through an elaborate ceremony every three to

Statue in the Bon
monastery at Kewzing

four years. Once initiated, the disciples are to practice the tantras diligently to attain Nirvana.

Legend has it that Padmasambhava was invited to assist a local prince who was thwarted by demons from building a gompa at Samye, in Tibet. Armed with his dorje (thunderbolt) he overcame the demons, completed the construction of the gompa and installed in it the first community of lamas. The native religion of Tibet was Bon and Padmasambhava was responsible for fusing this animistic set of beliefs and rituals with Buddhism, which resulted in the establishment of the Red Hat sect of Tibetan Buddhism. This later split into three main strands, the original known as the Nyingma, the Kargyu inspired by Gurus Naropa & Marpa and the Sakya by the Indian yogi Virupa. Reforms in the Red Hat sect resulted in the Gelugpa (Yellow Hat) sect becoming the dominant force from the sixteenth century onwards. Clashes between the two sects led to the Red Hats crossing into Sikkim and establishing the Buddhist monarchy as already described in the section on History ■

Mani stones adorn a wall at Tashiding

BODDHISATTAVAS

Boddhisattavas are beings who have attained enlightenment, but refusing to accept Nirvana choose to reincarnate so they can help release sentient beings caught in the cycle of suffering and rebirth. The Boddhisattava will not accept the reward of Nirvana till all beings have been led to enlightenment.

Some of the most revered Boddhisattavas are:

▸▸ MAITREYA

(Jampa in Tibetan), is the 'Buddha of the Future'. It is believed he will reappear on earth to restore the purity of the dharma, to deliver all sentient beings to enlightenment by revealing all that is hidden by ignorance and time. He is one Boddhisattava whose believers and devotees span both the Hinayana and Mahayana sects. He will be the last of five Buddhas to gain supreme enlightenment in this aeon. He is shown holding the stalk of a lotus in his hand and is depicted either sitting or standing.

▸▸ AVALOKITESWARA

(Gazing down Lord), embodies the compassion of all the Buddhas (karuna), and is regarded as the guardian of the country. The Dalai Lama and the Karmapa are considered living manifestations of Avalokiteswara. He is from the Lotus family and a family protector along with Manjusri and Vajrapani. His colouring symbolises passionate concern for beings and he is depicted either sitting in full lotus position or standing. He is shown with two, four or a thousand arms, being all-encompassing.

▸▸ PADMASAMBHAVA

(Guru Rinpoche), was a renowned Tantric saint from Northern India who brought Buddhism to Tibet. He is shown seated on a lotus, wearing a red cap and with his legs crossed. In his right hand he holds the vajra (thunderbolt) while the left rests on his lap.

▸▸ VAJRAPANI

He is a wrathful Boddhisattava and is one of the three protectors of the family, with Avalokiteswara and Manjusri. He fights a spiritual battle against forces of ignorance, craving and the samsara. He is depicted as a blue tantric figure with a flamed halo and wearing a garland of skulls and a wreath of snakes.

▸▸ MANJUSRI

(Prince of Wisdom) is a family protector, along with Avalokiteswara and Vajrapani. He represents wisdom, intelligence and confers mastery of dharma. Second only to Avalokiteswara, he is a very popular Boddhisattava and is shown holding the sword of truth in his right hand to cut through ignorance while the left hand is held out, palm forward, in the teaching mudra.

▸▸ GREEN TARA

She is the Boddhisattava of Compassion, gentle, heartfelt and born from the tears of Avalokiteswara. She protects and guides believers on the path of enlightenment and is often referred to as the Swift One due to her immediate response to prayers. She is the Wisdom Consort of Transcendental Buddha Amogasiddhi. She is portrayed with her left leg resting on the right thigh while the right leg steps forward gracefully in front of her. Her left hand is held in front of her heart, in the 'mudra of granting refuge' while the right hand rests on her knee in the 'mudra of generosity'.

▸▸ WHITE TARA

She is the Mother of all Buddhas and belongs to the Lotus family of Amitava. She energises those who visualise her to follow the spiritual path they have set out on. She is associated with health, strength and longevity and is shown sitting on a lotus and with seven eyes — the normal pair plus one in the center of the forehead in the 'third-eye' position and eyes on the palms of her hands and the soles of her feet.

THE WHEEL OF LIFE

The Wheel (Mandala) is a depiction of existence, with all its conditions and circumstances that is called samsara or sangsara – the unsatisfactory cycle of life, death and rebirth that can continue endlessly unless we work to change the situation. The Lord of Death, Yama, is depicted biting into the wheel and holding it firmly, implying that if the right path is not followed destruction will result.

The Hub contains the three poisons — lust or desire symbolised by the cock, aversion or hatred depicted by the snake, and the pig representing delusion or ignorance.

The Middle Ring, divided into six segments depicts the realms where all sentient beings are reborn.

Heaven is the divine realm and residence of Devas or Gods, who are born here by virtue of the good karma of meritorious deeds and charitable actions in previous lives. However, since enlightenment has not been attained they must continue on the Noble path, or risk leaving the realm after exhausting their good karma.

The Human realm is one of trial for humanity with good and evil influences co-existing.

The realm of Beasts is where those who have been cruel and have followed animal like instincts have been relegated to.

Hell is the darkest realm where those who harboured intense hatred are now tortured by scorching heat and icy cold.

Hungry Ghosts is the realm of those who are extremely selfish and even after death are consumed by desire—here they are in a constant state of hunger and thirst.

The Asuras is the realm of powerful entities who harbour hate and jealousy—they are anti-gods who are constantly at war. Having embarked on the Noble Path they failed to follow it completely and while attaining great power, their anger and envy deny them entrance to heaven while other merits keep them out of hell.

In each of the realms there is a Buddha in a different colour to guide one onto the Noble Path.

The Outermost Ring depicts the twelve karma formations or the links of interdependence. Enlightenment can only be attained by freeing oneself from all these formations.

The wheel shows the following labels: Craving, Clinging, Becoming, Feeling, Heaven, Rebirth, Contact, Humans, Asuras, Three Poisons, Old Age & Death, Six Senses, Beasts, Hungry Ghosts, Hell, Name & Form, Ignorance, Consciousness, Acts of Volition

Tangkha depicting the Wheel of Life in the 400-year-old Tawang Monastery, Arunachal

CHORTENS

In ancient times chortens, (Tibetan for stupas), were built as relic holders, but are now mainly built in honour of the Living Buddhas or Boddhisattavas. Chortens are shaped to symbolise the five elements of nature: Earth, Water, Fire, Air and Ether – which is the medium that the body converts to after death. The rectangular base represents the earth. The next, somewhat circular one, being water, the conical section symbolises fire, topped by a crescent representing air, with the oval right at the top being ether.

PRAYER FLAGS AND PRAYER WHEELS

Chortens are usually surrounded by prayer flags and prayer wheels. The flags are often white in colour, representing purity of thought and are supposed to carry the prayers of the faithful on the wings of wind.

Made of strips of cloth in oblong, rectangular or triangular shape, with holy inscriptions and lucky signs printed on them, these prayer flags are of four types. Those for luck are long narrow and oblong shaped victory banners and have a substantial amount of text on them, whereas others bear the symbol of the Dorje (Thunderbolt). The 'Wind Horse' flags depict a horse with a jewel on its back.

Prayer flags are an integral part of the landscape – on hilltops, trees and buildings.

Prayer wheels have holy mantras inscribed on them and rotating them brings a feeling of peace and tranquillity besides good luck. So go ahead and give those wheels a spin or buy your own personal handheld prayer wheel like those frequently seen in the hands of monks and other devotees. These are usually found in shops conveniently located near most gompas.

Phurba Chorten in Gangtok, Sikkim

EIGHT LUCKY SYMBOLS

Decorating gompas as well as various items of religious use, and others of tourist interest, you will notice eight symbols. These signs of the Buddhist faith symbolise the Eight Fold Path and are used as signs for good luck.

GOLDEN FISH
Represents the eyes of Buddha who, like the fish, could see through muddy waters. The pair represents the interdependence of the female and male.

PARASOL
Symbolises preservation and protection from harmful forces and negative energies.

VASE
Repository of fulfilment, long life, good health and prosperity.

ENDLESS KNOT
Represents Eternity and Unity – also called 'Mystic Dragon'.

LOTUS
Despite having its roots in dirt, the bloom is beautiful and represents purity of mind and body.

DHARMA WHEEL
Symbolises liberation from death and rebirth.

VICTORY BANNER
Triumph and victory of good over evil, as also over ignorance.

CONCH
Spread of dharma and awakening of sentient beings from their state of ignorance.

FESTIVALS

THE festivals reflect the intermingling of the three principal inhabitants' distinct cultures. Very few festivals, outside the three New Years, are exclusive to any community. The Nepalese follow the Hindu religion (Nepal is a Hindu kingdom) and hence the festivals are the same as those followed in the rest of India, though influence of the other cultures has led to some changes in the form of celebrations.

The Lepchas have their New Year known as Loosong or Namsoong and the Pang Lhabsol festival dedicated to Kanchendzonga. The bulk of the State's festivals relate to various aspects of Lord Buddha's life and

Festivities at Ralong Monastery

Tibetan Buddhism, with all communities participating.

Unfortunately as the following calendar shows, the main Buddhist festivals do not coincide with the 'ideal time' to visit Sikkim so if you want to enjoy the colourful and spectacular festival dances, a visit during the wetter or colder months is called for.

The main festivals are listed in chronological order but do remember to check for changes since they follow the lunar calendar.

▸▸ JAN–FEB: *Makar Sakranti* falls in mid-January and marks the fading away of the cold winter season.

Saraswati Puja is also observed by students in January.

Detor Chaam or the masked lama dance is held at the Enchey Gompa in Gangtok on the 18th/19th days of the 12th month of the Tibetan lunar calendar (TLC), and normally falls in January.

▸▸ MARCH: *Losar* is the Tibetan New Year and two days prior to it (generally early March) dances are performed at Rumtek and Pemayangtse Gompas.

Bhumchu, (which has been described earlier) is performed at Tashiding Gompa and devotees make offerings of flowers, fruits and butter lamps at Kechopari.

▸▸ MID–MARCH/MAY: The *International Flower Festival* showcases the pride of Sikkim's flora – orchids of innumerable hues as also gladioli, rhododendrons and magnolias. This wonderful array is on display at the Ridge in Gangtok.

▸▸ MAY: *Saga Dawa* is a triple blessed, three-in-one, festival to celebrate the birth of Lord Buddha, his attainment of Buddhahood, and subsequent Nirvana. Considered to be the holiest of the holy festivals, processions of monks carrying the sacred books are seen in Gangtok and other towns. The festival is held at the time of the full moon in the 4th lunar month and falls in late May or early June.

▸▸ JUNE: *Tse Chu Chaam* depicting the life of Guru Padmasambhava is held on the 10th day of the 5th lunar month and is one of Rumtek's premier attractions.

▸▸ JULY: *Drupka Teshi* is held to celebrate the day of the first teaching of the Four Noble Truths by Lord Buddha to his first five disciples at Sarnath. Prayers are held in the Deer Park at Gangtok on this day, which corresponds to the 4th day of the 6th lunar month of the Tibetan calendar.

▸▸ AUGUST: *Pang Lhabsol* was popularised by the third Chogyal of Sikkim and is indigenous to the State. The festival is dedicated to mighty Mt. Kanchendzonga, the presiding guardian deity. It also commemorates the Treaty of Brotherhood between the Lepchas and the Bhutias which was witnessed by the local deities. (Pang means witness). The festival is celebrated with the dramatic Warrior Dance and snowy Kanchendzonga is represented by a red mask ringed by five human skulls. Mahakala, the

protector of dharma, makes a dramatic entry and instructs Kanchendzonga to ensure that Sikkim remains prosperous and peaceful. The festival falls on the 15th day of the 7th lunar month (generally end August).

▸▸ OCTOBER: *Dassain* corresponds to Durga Puja or Dusshera and is followed by Tihar (Festival of Lights), a five-day celebration, which honours animals.

The first day is known as 'Kak Tihar', and is dedicated to crows who are offered rice. The second day is 'Kukkar Tihar' and marked by the garlanding of dogs. The third day corresponds with Diwali and is called 'Gai Tihar' – it is now the cows' turn and their horns are painted in bright colours. In the evening, lamps are lit, Lakshmi Puja is performed and in Gangtok, the central place of worship is the Durga Temple.

Lhabab Duchen celebrates the descent of Lord Buddha from the heavens. Legend has it that he went to heaven to pay homage to his mother Queen Mahamaya. While there he enthralled the Gods with his discourses, and they would not let him leave. After three months his followers on earth deputed Maugalayana to remind him to return to earth. The Gods only allowed this after being convinced that they could visit earth to listen to his discourses. Somewhat reluctantly the Gods allowed Lord Buddha to descend on a special 'triple ladder' built by Vishwakarma (the God of all things mechanical)

▶▶ DECEMBER: *The Kagyed Dance* held on the 28th/29th days of the 10th lunar month symbolises the victory of good over evil, with the evil spirits of the past year being exorcised and the good spirits of the New Year being welcomed. Archery contests and prayers precede the main dance which is performed at the Royal Chapel in Gangtok, as also the nearby Phodong Gompa and Pemayangtse in the West.

Loosong is the Sikkimese New Year which falls in December and is celebrated by the Sikkimese Bhutias.

Namsoong, also held at the same time, is celebrated by the Sikkimese Lepchas. Coinciding with the end of the harvest season it is also known as *Sonam Losar* (Farmers New Year) by the Lepchas ■

The patron saint, Guru Padmasambhava

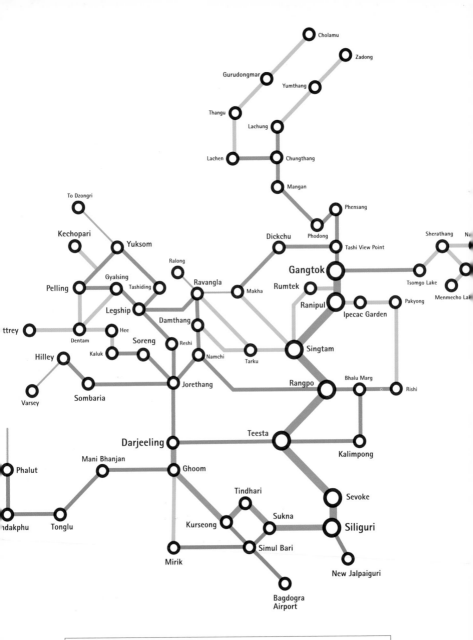

Cholamu

Zadong

Gurudongmar

Yumthang

Thangu

Lachung

Lachen

Chungthang

Mangan

To Dzongri

Phensang

Kechopari

Dickchu

Phodong

Sherathang

Na...

Yuksom

Ralong

Ravangla

Gangtok

Tashi View Point

Pelling

Gyalsing

Tashiding

Makha

Rumtek

Tsomgo Lake

Legship

Damthang

Ranipul

Ipecac Garden

Menmecho Lake

ttrey

Dentam

Hee

Reshi

Namchi

Singtam

Pakyong

Hilley

Kaluk

Soreng

Tarku

Varsey

Sombaria

Jorethang

Rangpo

Bhalu Marg

Rishi

Darjeeling

Teesta

Kalimpong

Phalut

Mani Bhanjan

Ghoom

Tindhari

Sevoke

ndakphu

Tonglu

Kurseong

Sukna

Siliguri

Mirik

Simul Bari

New Jalpaiguri

Bagdogra
Airport

National Highway in the plains

Wide enough for only two smaller vehicles to
cross, and a not-so-smooth surface.

Wide enough for two large vehicles to cross without
having to pull over and come to a halt; and a
generally good surface.

The width would be the same as above, but the
surface would be that of a lunar landscape, or
extremely stony.

Wide enough for a car/jeep to cross a large vehicle
like a bus with a generally good surface

THE HOLIDAY

*from now on, the author takes the steering
wheel and leads you through a most scenic
and spectacular land, with an itinerary
that unfolds over the next pages...*

TRAVEL PLAN

DAY 1
▸▸ **Rumtek**

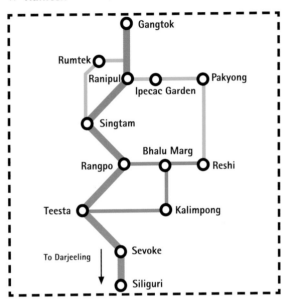

If you want to enjoy the sights of Gangtok but avoid the hustle bustle, Rumtek may be a better place to stay – it is close enough to Gangtok and much more relaxing.

Siliguri-Teesta	53 km	Singtam-Gangtok	39 km
Teesta-Rangpo	22 km		
Rangpo-Singtam	10 km		

Your Sikkim adventure begins in Rumtek, which is a three to four hour drive from Siliguri (see section on 'Getting There'). Approximately 12km short of Gangtok is a road leading down to the left and a short 12km drive through dense forest, brings you to your destination.

You will reach Rumtek late afternoon and we recommend walking to the old Rumtek Monastery, 2km from the entrance to the new main one. On your return, a kilometer short of the main monastery you can stop at the 'Ani Gompa', an all nuns monastery. Time permitting, you can visit the Nehru Botanical Garden with its large variety of plants and trees and exotic orchids ■

DAY 2
▶▶ Rumtek Monastery, Ipecac (Saramsa) Garden, and Pal Zurmang (Lingdum) Monastery

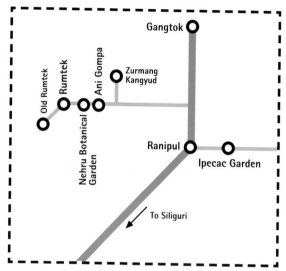

In the right season, Ipecac Garden is a perfect place to enjoy the beautiful flora for which Sikkim is famous.

Ranipul-Rumtek	12 km	Gangtok-Ipecac Garden	14 km
Rumtek-Gangtok	24 km	Ranipul-Gangtok	12 km
Gangtok-Zurmang Kagyud	20 km		

The day starts with a visit to the Rumtek Monastery, located on a hill facing Gangtok, twenty-four kilometers away.

This monastery is the seat of the Gyalwang Karmapa, the head of the Kagyupa order of Tibetan Buddhism.

What is immediately noticeable, and comes as a rude shock, is the presence of armed guards and pickets on the perimeter of this awesome building. The reasons for this are two-fold, but a brief historical interlude is necessary.

Lama Marpa, a disciple of the Indian Buddhist guru Naropa, founded the Kagyupa order in Tibet in the eleventh century. Legend has it that the first

Rumtek Monastery, the seat of the Karmapa

Karmapa spend several years meditating in a cave, and when he emerged, ten thousand fairies feted him and each offered a strand of hair. These were woven into a black hat, which has been handed down over generations, and popular belief suggests that unless enclosed or firmly held down it can fly away!

In 1959, following the Chinese invasion and

There is a variety of accommodation to choose from at Rumtek. You can stay for as little as Rs. 200 per night or in true luxury....

subsequent complete takeover of Tibet, the 16th Karmapa, Gyalwang Karmapa fled to Bhutan and was then invited by the Chogyal to settle permanently in Sikkim. After spending some time at the Phodong Monastery, construction on the permanent seat of the Karmapa started at Rumtek in 1962. Following a meeting with Pt. Nehru, the work received an impetus and with assistance

While visiting Rumtek, do not miss the temple dedicated to Tara — it is located adjacent to the main building.

forthcoming from both, the Indian authorities and Sikkimese monarchy, the monastery was completed in 1966. The 16th Karmapa passed away in 1981 and it is in the present time that controversial elements have arisen.

As is the norm, the 16th Karmapa is believed to have left instructions in a sealed box describing where and how his 'tulku', or reincarnation, could be identified. Following these directions, Ogyen

Drodul Trinley Dorje was found in a remote corner of eastern Tibet in 1992, and with the blessings of the Chinese government, installed as the 17th Karmapa at the traditional main seat at Tsurphu. However, a second candidate was discovered in Bhutan and a certain section of mainly Bhutanese monks believe him to be the true 'tulku'. However, having received the blessings of the Dalai Lama, for all intents and purposes, Ogyen Dorje is

The Great Kings of the Four Cardinal Directions at Rumtek

THE 17TH KARMAPA

The 17th Gyalwang Karmapa was born to a nomadic family in the Lhotak region of eastern Tibet in 1985. A cuckoo landed on the tent he was born in and a mysterious conch-like sound was heard by many throughout the valley. Such events portend the birth of an enlightened teacher. However, in 1992, he asked his family to shift and to expect a visit from travelling monks. Shortly after they had set up their new home, and pursuant to instructions left with the followers of the 16th Karmapa, Apo Gaga was discovered to be the 17th Karmapa. The 16th Karmapa had predicted his own departure from Tsurphu Monastery and also had said he would return – which happened in September 1992 when the 17th Karmapa was enthroned. The ceremony was with the permission of the Chinese authorities and attended by 20,000 followers. At Tsurphu, the Karmapa embarked on a course of religious studies but as the years went by, he came under increasing pressure to act in a manner contrary to his obligations as the Karmapa. He publicly refused to denounce the Dalai Lama and finally in 1999, recognising that his usefulness in Tibet was being undermined, he decided to leave. He and a handful of loyal attendants concocted a bold scheme to escape and in December 1999 the fourteen-year old Karmapa pretended to enter into solitary retreat. Borrowing from the best of Bollywood themes, donning civilian garb, he slipped out through a window and using a combination of foot, horseback, motor vehicles and even helicopter by way of transportation, he managed to arrive safely in Dharamsala in January 2000. He was accorded refugee status by the Government of India in 2001 but continues to live near Dharamsala awaiting permission to take over his traditional seat at Rumtek.

acknowledged as the 17th Karmapa.

The threat of a rival take-over still remains – hence the presence of armed guards!

The second controversy arose from 1999 onwards, when the 17th Karmapa, having lived in Tibet with official Chinese patronage, 'escaped' to India much like his predecessor and the Dalai Lama. Suspicions that he is a 'Chinese plant' have not been fully allayed in the corridors of the Indian government and he is not being given permission to take up residence in Rumtek. This explains the many posters and wall graffiti asking the government to 'Bring Home the Karmapa'.

Rumtek Monastery, though modern, is a replica of the original in Tibet. It is located around two kilometers from the earlier Rumtek Monastery that

The Rumtek Monastery complex

A novice at Rumtek

was built in 1730 by the 4th Chogyal, under the guidance of the 9th Karmapa, but was destroyed by fire.

The monastery – World Dharma Chakra Center – became the international center of the Kagyupas during the 16th Karmapa's reign. A new generation of Kagyupa masters are being trained here in the traditional study and meditation practices that originated 800 years ago. The complex exemplifies the traditional Tibetan style and this three-storied edifice is the largest monastery in Sikkim. The ground floor encompasses the prayer hall while the first floor was the living quarter of the 16th Karmapa and the top floor is a terrace with a small stupa. A three meter tall gold plated statue of Lord Buddha dominates the main prayer hall. Hundreds of miniature Buddhas, kept in glass fronted pigeon holes, represent the 'Buddhas in the making'.

In the entrance hall to the prayer room are wall paintings of the Great Kings of the Four Cardinal Directions who guard the Universe from demons. From left to right they are – the King of the East with a white face and playing a musical instrument; the King of the North, with a blue face, fangs and drawing a sword from its scabbard; the King of the West with a blood red face, a serpent coiled on his arm, and holding a stupa in his hand; and the King of the South with a yellow face holding a rat and a banner.

If it's a clear day a picnic lunch would be the preferred option. In these beautiful environs, you can find a scenic spot whenever you are hungry!

The walls are embellished with paintings in vibrant colours as well as beautiful tangkhas. An array of tubular silk banners contributes to the uplifting ambience of the monastery.

In the adjacent building, to the left of the main one, is a temple on the first floor dedicated to the Goddess Tara that should not be missed.

Behind the main prayer hall is the Great Golden Relinquary Stupa of the 16th Karmapa, which contains his bones and ashes. Along the walls are statues of his fifteen predecessors – the rotating paper prayer wheels, which derive their motion from the heat of butter lamps, add to the air of peace and tranquillity. The lower section houses a wooden block printing press where prayer books and prayer flags, made from handmade paper, are printed and these are for sale.

Opposite this stupa is the Karmae Nalanda Institute of Buddhist Studies that has an enormous portrait of Lord Buddha at the entrance. A short distance up the hill is the Hermitage where monks go into seclusion for periods up to three years!

Of the many devotional religious dances or 'chaams' held here the main is the Tse Chu which is held in June/July every year and depicts events in the life of Guru Padmasambhava. Kagyed, the traditional sacred lama dance of Mahakala, the protector, marks the end of the Tibetan year in February-March. The celebration of the New Year typically involves Tibetan opera dance performances, which continue up to eight days.

Allow yourself a couple of hours to explore and admire this magnificent monastery and if perchance your timing is right and you are there during a prayer service, do sit in as the deep resonating chants and the rhythmic beating of drums is a spiritually moving experience.

If you are driving your own vehicle, expect to be confounded by a plethora of 'one way', 'no entry' and 'no parking' zones within Gangtok!

Head back to your hotel for lunch or carry a picnic basket to your next destination –the Ipecac Garden which is 17km (30 mins) away.

Located on a six acre spread, this garden has an amazing variety of orchid species as well as interesting medicinal plants like the ipecac, from which the garden gets its name. Some varieties of butterflies, that Sikkim is so famous for, can easily be spotted here. If you are in luck, you may chance upon the endangered 'Golden Birdwing', whose existence is in as much peril as the Royal Bengal tiger.

While returning to your hotel at Rumtek, visit the Pal Zurmang Kagyud Monastery at Lingdum, a four kilometer drive on the road leading to Ranka. Though of recent origin (1995), the complex is a fine example of Tibetan monastic architecture.

If you are spending the night in Gangtok, the order of your sight seeing schedule will need to be reversed ■

DAY 3
⏵⏵ Gangtok sightseeing

Gangtok (population 50,000) is the capital of
Sikkim and lies at a comfortable altitude of
5500ft/1675m. Gangtok, meaning 'high hill', is
spectacularly located midst emerald-hued terraces
of paddy, overlooking deep, rich valleys and offers
an amazing view of the snow capped Himalayas.
However, do not carry visions of a quaint,
picturesque hill station – put bluntly, Gangtok is a
built up township but serves very well as a base
as also a conduit point.

There are, however, quite a few 'local attractions'
in and around Gangtok, which you can visit
leisurely, or at a fast pace, depending on how
much time you are spending here.

**White Hall, former
residence of the
commissioner**

View of Mt. Kanchendzonga from Gangtok

As a visitor, the first thing you notice is the overall cleanliness and strong sense of civic awareness that you encounter, not just in Gangtok but even the smaller destinations and stops on your journey – pleasantly clean roadside eateries and to your great relief, clean facilities too! A step further and certainly a welcome surprise is the success that Gangtok has had in declaring the city a 'polythene-free zone'. There is no evidence of that careless hand, casually extended out of the car, dropping a crumpled bag of something – in

Gangtok has several good restaurants and we recommend trying Bakers Café, Blue Sheep, Hotels Tashi Delek and Tibet.

fact, litter is almost unseen and garbage bins are generously provided through the city.

People are unfailingly courteous and helpful and there is an evident orderliness on the roads. Since the roads are narrow, there are no public buses, but jeeps and vans ply convenient routes and stop at well-chosen locations. Traffic is disciplined; so do not expect them to stop at whim — or on demand — anywhere other than their designated stop (if only this would happen to us in Delhi!).

The Research Institute of Tibetology, is located

You may want to hire a taxi for half a day to take you to the more distant places such as the Zoological Park, Ganesh Tok and Enchey Gompa.

midst a small forest of oak, magnolia and birch trees, and was built in 1958 in the traditional Tibetan style. It promotes research of Mahayana Buddhism as also of the language and traditions of Tibet and houses one of the world's largest collections of texts and documents on Buddhism. The manuscripts are mainly in the form of

The Phurba Chorten in Gangtok

xylographs, an ancient method of printing using wooden slats with the matter embossed in reverse. There is also a museum that contains antique coins and statues, as also exquisite 'tangkhas' (silk scrolls with art painted on them) depicting the eight manifestations of Guru Padmasambhava (Guru Rinpoche), the founder of Tibetan

Buddhism. There are relics of monks from King Ashoka's time, masks, sacred and ceremonial objects such as the 'kapali', a bowl made from a human skull and the 'varku', a flute made from the thighbone.

The Chogyal Palden Thondup Namgyal Memorial Park, which is just below the Institute, is a peaceful place for a quiet walk or to pull out a book and spend time reading in this sylvan oasis in the heart of the city.

Around five hundred meters from the Institute, on top of a small hillock, is the huge Do-Drul (Phurba) Chorten. This white stupa with its gold apex was built in the 1940s by the head of the Nyingma order, Trul Shik Rinpoche, and the then Chogyal, Tashi Namgyal. Visible from many parts of Gangtok, this chorten is supposed to invoke the gods to maintain peace and tranquillity in the state. Surrounded by 108 small prayer wheels with the mystic mantra "Om Mane Padme Hum" (Hail Jewel in the Lotus) inscribed in Tibetan, the chorten also contains a complete set of Kanjur, the holy books with teachings of Lord Buddha. A smaller chorten next to it contains huge images of Guru Padmasambhava and his incarnation Guru Snang Sid Zilzam.

From here one can drive past the building housing the Sikkim Legislature, onto the main Secretariat Complex and the nearby park presided over by a large statue of Lord Buddha in the teaching position, a replica of the one in Sarnath. The statue, which is surrounded by exotic flowers, has a butter lamp that is always kept alight before it.

Proceed to the Ridge and visit the building where a perennial flower show is on view. Usually there is a fantastic array of the varied flora of the state, with particular emphasis on the exotic

The Ridge is a great area to stretch your legs and enjoy being in the city, away from the hustle bustle of M.G. Road.

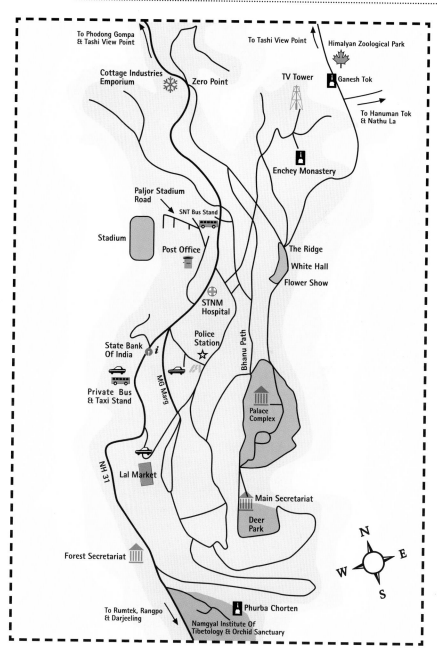

To Phodong Gompa
& Tashi View Point

To Tashi View Point

Himalyan Zoological Park

Cottage Industries
Emporium

Zero Point

TV Tower

Ganesh Tok

To Hanuman Tok
& Nathu La

Enchey Monastery

Paljor Stadium
Road

SNT Bus Stand

Stadium

Post Office

The Ridge

White Hall

Flower Show

STNM
Hospital

Police
Station

Bhanu Path

State Bank
Of India

MG Marg

Private Bus
& Taxi Stand

Palace
Complex

NH 31

Lal Market

Main Secretariat

Deer
Park

Forest Secretariat

To Rumtek, Rangpo
& Darjeeling

Phurba Chorten

Namgyal Institute Of
Tibetology & Orchid Sanctuary

N
W   E
S

The Ridge in Gangtok

orchid. At one end of the Ridge is the gate to the Royal Palace, now no longer occupied. Within the palace compound is the Tsukhlakhang or Royal Chapel where the Chogyals were coronated and royal wedding ceremonies were performed. This was the seat of power, but today it conveys a sad sense of desolation of an era gone by—except for the time during the Sikkimese New Year, (Loosong, which falls in December), when it is open to the public and ceremonies that hark to the old days are performed. At the other end of the Ridge is the 'White Hall' built back in 1932 in memory of the first political officer Claude White. Close by is the chief minister's official residence, Mintogang which interprets as 'hilltop crowned with blossoms'.

We can now move up to the two-hundred year old Enchey Gompa, an important seat of the Nyingma order. It was built in 1901 on a site chosen by Lama Druptab Karpu, a tantric monk who is believed to have harnessed his mystic powers to fly – or at least to levitate! The prayer hall is a riot of colour with the large Buddha at the altar or 'chwa shyam', flanked by Guru Padmasambhava on the right and Avalokiteswara (Chenresig) on the left. There is a fearsome image of Dorje Phurba or 'Vajra Kila'; Dorje the wild eyed male part of the image holding Phurba, the female part, in his embrace and crushing a demon with his talons. Images of the Great Kings of the Four Cardinal Directions, who protect not only the gompa but the Universe from demons, are to be seen in the vestibule.

For those interested in wildlife, the Himalayan Zoological Park offers a view of local species like the red panda, Himalayan black bear, barking and musk deer and various other animals held in open-air enclosures. As far as zoos go this is one of the best vis-a-vis its expanse and openness. Spending a few pleasant, peaceful hours walking the wooded paths and viewing animals in relatively natural surroundings can be considered time well spent.

Ask your driver to head for Ganesh Tok. This small, quaint, unspoilt temple dedicated to Lord Ganesh is near the entrance to the Zoological Park and from here you have a panoramic view of Gangtok and the Raj Bhawan complex. If you are in luck, on the opposite side, you will get a breathtaking view of the major peaks on the

The Sikkim Tourism Office is conveniently located on M.G. Road. They are extremely courteous and if you need assistance this is where you should go.

GOMPAS

The Gompa, or Solitary Place, was the building where monks could isolate themselves from the world to further their meditative process. Gompas were therefore built in remote locations. Their concept can be traced to the caves, hollowed out of sheer rock, which were used by monks for retreat and meditation during the time of Gautam Buddha. The growing acceptance of Buddhism, and the patronage it received from the state, led to gompas evolving into large, magnificent edifices that served both as places of worship for devotees and also as residences and teaching centers for monks. Each gompa held its own treasure of holy relics. According to a scriptural couplet, the gompa should be built with its back to the hill face and the front facing a water body. The approach to all gompas is lined with rows of fluttering prayer flags, gleaming white chortens and mani (medong) walls.

To this day people choose mani stones, preferably beautiful and unusual ones, and etch them, in the graceful Tibetan calligraphy, with mantras - the most common being "Om Mane Padme Hum". The stones are piled on each other and form walls of prayer. Local belief holds that picking and carrying away one of these offerings of prayer brings bad luck.

Inside a gompa, one first enters the 'chukhong' or assembly hall, where monks are found engaged in various rituals or in chanting prayers. The most sacred area of the gompa is the 'lhakhang', literally 'god's room', where the central deity with his

attendant images is enshrined. Butter lamps provide beautiful, soft illumination and the walls are adorned with a variety of paintings and tangkhas. The interiors are vibrant with rich colours and the glowing images of Lord Buddha and the Boddhisattavas. Being centers of learning, most gompas have extensive libraries, with xylographs of the 'Kanjur' (holy book of Buddha's teachings) and the 'Thanjur' (commentaries on the teachings).

Depending on the time of day, a gompa can be a beehive of activity but the overall aura is one of peace and tranquillity.

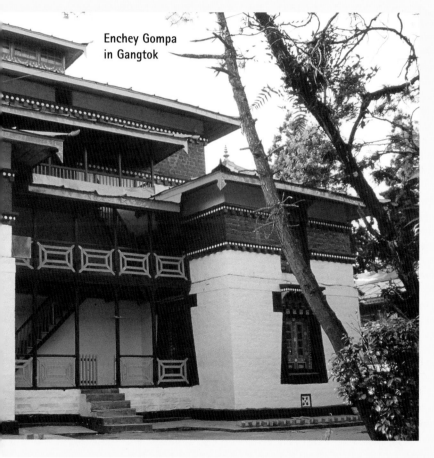

Enchey Gompa in Gangtok

western border. The peaks are regarded as sacred by the Sikkimese and most have remained unscaled. Kanchendzonga, (House of Five Treasures - kept by the Gods on the summit), has been scaled a few times but even here the climbers returned a few feet short of the summit in deference to local sentiments. Kanchendzonga is considered Sikkim's guardian deity with its five peaks forming a hand, held upright, and blessing the state perpetually. In the words of Lama Lhatsun Chembo, "The peak most conspicuously gilded by the rising sun is the treasury of gold; the peak that remains in cold grey shade is the storehouse for silver; and the other peaks are

The Five Treasures of Kanchendzonga viewed from Pemayangtse, W. Sikkim

vaults for gems, grains and the holy books".

If the day is clear, drive to the Tashiding View Point, which provides an excellent panoramic view of the western peaks, including the majestic Mt. Kanchendzonga. Later, if you still have the energy, or 'dum', for more, wander around Lal Bazaar, the local market with a distinct flavour of its own. It is a hub of activity, combining and integrating the past with the present and the rural with the urban – particularly on the 'Haat', or market day, on Sundays.

Remember to have a reasonably early dinner as the next day involves leaving at 6.00 a.m. which for many of us is a really early start! ■

You definitely want to make an early start as Tsomgo Lake is a truly beautiful sight under clear skies, as is Menmecho Lake.

DAY 4
▶▶ **Tsomgo Lake, Nathu La & Menmecho Lake**

Nathu La

Sherathang

Kupup

Karponang

Kyongnosla Sanctuary

Tsomgo Lake

Gangtok

Hanuman Tok

Baba Harbhajan Mndir

Menmecho Lake

Permits to visit Nathu La are granted to only forty vehicles in a day so ensure your tour operator does not leave things to the last minute.

Gangtok-Karponang	15 km	Tsomgo Lake-Sherathang	12 km
Karponang-Tsomgo Lake	19 km	Sherathang-Nathu La	05 km
Tsomgo-Menmecho Lake	20 km		

On this day you are heading into high altitudes and should aim to be out of the hotel by 6 a.m. to avoid encountering inclement weather that usually sets in by the late afternoon.

Visits to Nathu La are only possible three days of the week and you should ensure your travel agent factored this in while planning the itinerary.

You will need to carry warm clothes for the day and the best way to equip yourself is by 'layering' your clothing — ending up with a warm, wind-proof parka. Closed shoes and warm socks are also essential.

Ask your driver to take you on a 2km detour, off the main road, to Hanuman Tok (7200ft/2200m).

There is a spectacular view of the snow peaks from here and sunrise is a particularly good time for viewing. While Ganesh Tok is a small, quaint temple perched atop a hill and can hold only a couple of devotees at a time, Hanuman Tok is a much larger, modern construction. Just before the temple site is the cremation ground of the royal family of Sikkim. The area is studded with chortens marking the exact cremation spot of various family members.

Having resumed your journey, you will ascend quite steeply to Karponang, which is only 15km from Gangtok but at an altitude of almost 10,000ft/3050m. Around nine kilometers up the road, there is a good view of Gangtok and the surrounding hills.

Tsomgo Lake

After a short drive of another 10km, you are at a little over 12,000ft/3650m, and crest a ridge to have Tsomgo Lake unfold before you. This serene lake, one kilometer long and fifteen meters deep, remains frozen during the winter months till mid-March. Between May and August, it is possible to see rhododendrons, primulas, poppies and irises in full bloom.

An ATM at 13,200 ft! The coolest cash you can lay your hands on!

Above the 15th kilometer Sikkim Police check post, lies the high altitude Kyongnosla Alpine Sanctuary where the blood pheasant and red panda can be spotted.

You can stop to drink in the view and also a cuppa tea, or breakfast. Coming in early, you hopefully miss the crowds that begin to build up as the day warms up. The 'dhabas' surrounding

Carry a packed lunch, as the fare on offer at Tsomgo is not particularly appealing.

It is very cold at Nathu La. Carry a thermos of tea — you will need it to help you thaw out on the way down!

the lake can soon resemble Mumbai's Chowpatty Beach on a good day — specially on Sundays when domestic visitors to the Baba Harbhajan Singh Temple add to the tourist crowd!

The best option, of course, would be to carry a packed breakfast and a flask of tea or coffee, locate a peaceful, picturesque spot and enjoy a 'scenic breakfast' in privacy! Look out for brahmany ducks on the streams leading into the lake as you drive on.

Almost 5km up the road, you will come across a sight that certainly deserves a place in the Guinness

Book of Records. There is an ATM at 13,200ft run by UTI Bank—so carry your ATM cards and make a withdrawal of 'high value, cool cash'!! Do not miss the computerised railway-booking center on the opposite side which must be another 'first'.

Your next stop is Sherthang, an army check point 12km from Tsomgo Lake and 5km short of Nathu La, where the army withholds all cameras; to be collected on your return. Nathu La, at 14,400ft/4400m, is the only place where you can almost rub noses with Chinese soldiers across the international border!

Frozen mosaic — the river en route to Nathu La

Prior to the 1962 invasion by China, this was the major pass linking Sikkim with Tibet, and the road snaking down to Yuthang in the Chumbi valley is quite visible in clear weather. After a skirmish in 1967, there have been no military clashes on this border and in fact every Thursday, one can witness the exchange of mail between the Indian and Chinese border authorities.

It is an extremely humbling experience to see first hand the difficult conditions the army – both enlisted men and officers – live and operate in, on our Himalayan borders. Nathu La is blanketed in snow for up to nine months of the year – there is no electricity in the living quarters, which are literally snow-covered bunkers. Electricity by diesel generator sets is used only during meal times and for the weekly movie. A typical posting ranges from six months up to eighteen months. The weather is extremely harsh and cases of electrocution during frequent thunderstorms, often accompanied by fearsome bolts of lightening, are not uncommon. The lack of action, for many, is another negative factor – some actually expressed the feeling that Siachen is a comparatively better posting as any action was preferable to the mind-numbing tedium of just surviving in a cold and dark bunker! One can only be awestruck by the perseverance of these fellow human beings!

Since it is freezing cold and walking is a strain at this altitude, make a quick visit to the memorial and attempt a glimpse of the Chinese soldiers often visible on the other side of the barbed wire boundary. Then descend to the last stop of the day – Menmecho Lake – with one possible short stop on the way to catch up on the legend of Baba Harbhajan.

Make sure your driver knows that you plan to visit Menmecho Lake as a separate permit may be required. Given the poor state of the track to the lake, don't let this be a spur-of-the-moment decision.

THE LEGEND OF BABA HARBHAJAN

A touching and little-known task performed by the army in the snowy wilderness, five kilometers from the Tibet border, is to maintain – officially - the shrine of one of its soldiers who drowned while on duty in 1968.

To this day, Sepoy Harbhajan Singh, of 23 Punjab, has his service roll number on the payrolls, as he not only 'guards' the border but also heals ailments of fellow 'faujis' and civilians alike. His salary is sent to his mother and each year a rail reservation is booked to facilitate his 'home leave'!

Harbhajan was only nineteen when he went missing while leading a pack of mules from his battalion to remote, high altitude locations that had previously seen intense action during the Indo-Chinese war in 1962. He is said to have appeared in a dream to his senior colleague, identifying the exact location they would find his body and his rifle and asking them to build a shrine there for him. It is claimed the dream was precise and having located his remains, his colleagues in the regiment believed it auspicious to honour his request and felt his spirit would protect them always. Over the years, this shrine has acquired the status of a place of pilgrimage and both army as well as civilian visitors throng to it. On Sundays, a 'langar' is organised and free lunch provided to all visitors.

A contemporary touch to this devotion is the stacks of mineral water bottles left for a week, with names labelled on them, to be taken as 'prasad', which is said to remove not only pain but also stress. School children from Gangtok and around leave their textbooks here to be blessed when exam-fever and stress take over. These offerings are placed next to the ante-room that holds 'Baba's' uniform; his shirt epaulets now bear badges of a honorary captain — as high a rank as a sepoy can hope to be promoted to!

MENMECHO LAKE

After this short break, it is a 2.5km descent to the lake, which is the source of the River Rangopocha – a tributary of the Teesta. Like Tsomgo, this lake is also fed by snowmelt from the surrounding mountains but is much larger in size and also holds a considerable trout population. The drive down to Menmecho is along a rock strewn rough path that is quite steep in places. Few people seem to make the effort to get to the lake so it retains a certain air of mystery and timelessness. It is surrounded by

Menmecho Lake, below the Baba Harbhajan Temple

a rich, varied forest and some rather interesting rock formations. Compared to the much developed, hustle bustle of Tsomgo Lake, the tranquillity of Menmecho makes the visit an almost spiritual experience!

After lunch, and a beer if the sun is still out, head back as it can suddenly turn overcast and it rains in the afternoons more often than not. It is best to start your return journey by 3 p.m. with a farewell chai (or coffee) break at Tsomgo, before you return to Gangtok for a well-deserved rest and a good dinner ■

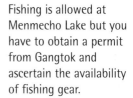

Fishing is allowed at Menmecho Lake but you have to obtain a permit from Gangtok and ascertain the availability of fishing gear.

DAY 5
▸▸ Drive to Lachen/Lachung

To Gurudongmar Lake

Lachung

Lachen   Chungthang

Naga Waterfall

Singit View Point

Mangan

Namok   Mayank Chu   Phensang

Phodong

Kabi Longstok

Tashi View Point

Gangtok

Meals will be basic till you return to Gangtok so carry supplementary 'goodies'! Chungthang is the last place to make phone calls but don't count on the lines working!

Gangtok-Phensang	31 km	Mangan-Chungthang	30 km
Phensang-Phodong	09 km	Chungthang-Lachen	27 km
Phodong-Mangan	25 km	Chungthang-Lachung	21 km

From now on, for the next two to three nights, you will be living in relatively spartan conditions. The food will be simple but wholesome and accommodation, though clean and comfortable, has none of the trappings of luxury that Gangtok and some of the other towns offer – just grand, awe-inspiring vistas that Nature lays on for your viewing pleasure!

After crossing Gangtok and the Tashi View Point, the road leads you to either Lachen or Lachung via Mangan and Chungthang. Twenty kilometers from Gangtok, you pass Kabi Longstok, the historic place where the treaty between the Lepcha king Thekong Tek and the Bhutia chieftain Khye

Bumsa was signed in the fifteenth century.

At Phensang, the monastery originally built in 1721 has been renovated and is worth a stop as its remoteness and isolation lends it a very peaceful aura. Approximately three kilometers out of Phensang, a stop at the Mayank Chu waterfall is a

The waterfall at Mayank Chu

A Lepcha woman taking
shelter during a passing
storm

must. A stairway and viewing platform has been built and the climb is well worth the effort as what appears to be a small but powerful waterfall then reveals four distinct levels of falls! Stop at the picturesque hamlet of Namok (an hour and a half away from Gangtok), where a wholesome lunch can be enjoyed at either the Silver Peak Restaurant or Hotel Mystic Himalayan. Wander around and look for what may sound like cattle bells and you will find three prayer wheels rotating by an ingenious, water powered device (a simple turbine).

Further on, just before Singhit, is another large water driven prayer wheel and this spot also affords great mountain views. After you cross the Teesta, 14km before Chungthang and 2km before Tong, is the Naga waterfall which has such a powerful flow that the water has had to be channelled through and seems to literally cannon out of the mountainside – we privately termed it 'the shooter'!!

It is advisable to take a good long walk at Lachen, drink plenty of water and avoid alcohol this evening.

At Chungthang (altitude 5200ft/1600m), where the Lachen Chu (Teesta) and the Lachung Chu converge, a short visit is definitely recommended to the place where Guru Nanak rested while on his epic Himalayan odyssey. Communications from here on are practically non-existent, except through the auspices of army outposts in case of emergency; so take the opportunity to make your phone calls.

From here it is a short ascending drive to either Lachen (27km) or Lachung (21km), both of which are at around 9000ft/2750m, in beautiful, almost enchanted valleys. Enjoy an evening stroll and a visit to the monasteries in each place is a possible diversion. If you are at Lachen en route to Gurudongmar Lake, remember the next day calls for an early six o'clock start ■

GURU NANAK'S TRAVELS

Guru Nanak, the founder of the Sikh religion, was born in 1469. Auspicious signs accompanied his birth and the family pandit prophesied that he would become a great teacher. There were no signs of this in his childhood and as per custom, he was married at the age of sixteen and took employment as a storekeeper in the state granary. After having worked for twelve years, he was falsely accused of embezzlement. Always spiritually inclined by nature, while this experience left him sad and disillusioned, it also made him introspect deeply, seeking a greater reality. He is said to have received the divine command to forsake worldly life and speak a new language — one not of religious insularity but of tolerance and pluralism. He left his home and family of two children and became an itinerant preacher, travelling widely over the Punjab and North India. At this time the Bhakti, or devotional, movement was sweeping across the North and West of India, challenging the rigidity of both Hinduism and Islam. Nanak gradually acquired followers or 'shishyas', the vernacular form of 'sikhyas'. This led to the new thought being termed Sikhism and its followers Sikhs.

The rock has a hidden source of water that is regarded as 'amrit'

Besides North India, Guru Nanak visited Mecca, the center of Islam. According to legend, when confronted by a Qazi who found him sleeping with his feet pointed towards Kaaba, the holy shrine, Nanak's rejoinder was to ask the Qazi to point his feet in any direction where there was no God!

He is also believed to have travelled to Tibet to study the Buddhist beliefs but there is no definitive historical record of the journey. However, the ground evidence and revelations from Tibetan monks seemingly confirm the hypothesis – the question is whether he travelled to Lhasa via Ladakh or through Sikkim, crossing into Tibet over the Donkhya Nankund pass just above Gurudongmar Lake. As per local belief Nanak did indeed visit Tibet and the route was via Chungthang...

Midst a gentle green valley, protected by a low wall built by the villagers, lies a small compound now maintained by the army. Within this compound is a single hard-stone mound, 30ft high and 200ft in circumference, wherein lies a cave, the mouth of which is now walled up with stones. On top of the mound, there are several depressions that are believed to be the footprints of Guru Nanak and on the side, a few feet above the ground level, is a deep crevice filled with trickling water that is said to be a perennial flow. The legend, passed on through the ages and as told to us, is that Guru Nanak on his way to Tibet stayed here in the cave and since the water from the river was very muddy, 'produced' clean water, tapping into subterranean water veins in the mound. This is now treated as 'amrit', or holy water, and offerings of coins and flowers are to be found on top of the mound even though there is no priest in sight — only a Sikh gentleman from the army acts as guardian to the shrine. It is also said that the Guru was carrying rice packed in a banana leaf and seeing this the locals voiced their desire to grow good rice since it was a preferred cereal but didn't grow well in their region. Guru Nanak is said to have blessed his own rice and scattered it in the field adjoining this shrine — needless to say, this rice took root and from this field the locals spread it to others and the area now grows plentiful rice as also bananas. Even today, the original 'blessed rice' field is common village land protected by a wall enclosure.

All this is in the realm of legend and not historical fact, and another belief attributes this story of Chungthang, as well as the one you will be told later at Gurudongmar Lake, to Guru Rinpoche during his travel to Tibet via Sikkim in the eighth century.

DAY 6
▶▶ **Gurudongmar Lake and transit to Lachung via Chungthang**

Carry plenty of water and some Paracetemol from your travel kit. However, don't worry; you will be at the rarefied altitude of 16,000+ ft for only a few hours.

Cholamu Lake ○

Gurudongmar Lake ○   Yumthang ○

Thangu ○

Lachung ○

Lachen ○   ○ Chungthang

Chungthang-Lachung	21 km	Lachen-Thangu	28 km
Lachung-Yumthang	24 km	Thangu-Gurudogmar Lake	32 km
Chungthang-Lachen	27 km	Gurudogmar-Cholamu Lake	09 km

The next day requires an early start as you do not want to run into rough weather at over 17,000ft/5200m! Ensure an intake of atleast one to two litres of water (as advised in the section on Acute Mountain Sickness), since you will ascend to 17,300ft in just two and a half hours.

The drive is scenically varied and beautiful, climbing through verdant forests with the Lachen Chu (Teesta), rushing alongside the road from Chungthang onwards. Snow mountain peaks are visible above the forest and the morning light filtering through the valley creates an effect that

mere words cannot hope to capture. You should pause for as many 'photo-ops' as you like, since in all likelihood you will not be allowed to carry cameras beyond a particular army check post. An hour long drive, covering twenty-eight kilometers, brings you to the army camp at Thangu (14,000ft/4250m). Thangu is the base for trekking up to the Green Lake (now partially dried up). It is a reasonably large army camp that serves as a base for border outposts lying beyond Gurudongmar Lake. If you have activated any army contacts, a hot 'chai' break at the army mess is a welcome stop but your own stocks in a thermos will do just as nicely.

Approximately 3km out of Thangu, all signs of

The peak, named 'Raja' by the army — a little after Thangu

vegetation disappear and you are well above the tree line, surrounded by glacial (perennial) snow peaks on either side. From verdant lush green the transformation to a snowy desert is awesome and the short journey of 32km (about 1.5 hours), to the lake is breathtaking – in more ways than one at this height!! Even though the ascent is gradual, your vehicle moves slowly as it too seems to be struggling for air while climbing on to the Tibetan plateau. You now face miles of flat, brown terrain speckled with snow and have by now traversed the Himalayas and are literally, 'on the other side'. In this arid countryside, a sudden flash of colour

Gurudongmar Lake

startles the eye as prayer flags appear in the distance, fluttering briskly in the wind and marking the location of the lake. After cresting a large 'sand dune' you come upon Gurudongmar Lake nestled like a jewel amid crested peaks!

While some attribute the legend of Gurudongmar Lake to Guru Nanak, others refer it to Guru Rinpoche. Legend has it that the lake remained frozen most of the year and hence it was not possible to use it as a source of water. When Guru Nanak/Guru Rimpoche passed by on his way to Tibet, the locals approached him appealing for help with water and from then on, the part of the lake that the Guru bathed in does not freeze while the rest ices over. Hence, this water is regarded as 'amrit'. The lake is gaily edged with numerous multi-coloured Tibetan prayer flags and irrespective of religious belief, people collect bottles of this 'blessed' water for themselves. A small stream that emanates from the lake joins one originating from the nearby Cholamu Lake and builds up into the Lachen Chu (Teesta).

Despite the fact that you may be feeling fit, do not let the beauty of the lake entice you to undertake any vigorous physical activity.

If you have secured permission from the army, it may be possible to drive 6-8km further to a camp at 18,000ft/5500m, near the border with China. Our armed forces occupy the high peaks with some outpost bunkers located as high as 22,000ft – an altitude even higher than the deadly Siachen Glacier. What is truly amazing is the sight of small battle tanks stationed here. Being a plateau, this is the only place in the world that tanks can operate at such high altitudes and be used to guard the border.

Remember to keep drinking lots of water even on the return journey back to Lachen for a late, but very welcome, hot lunch. You should then proceed to Lachung via Chungthang, a drive of 48km that should take you a couple of hours ■

DAY 7
▸▸ Lachung – a visit to the 'Valley of Flowers' and Yumthang

To Cholamu Lake

Donkiala Pass ○

○ Zadong

Yumthang ○

Lachung ○

○ Mt.Katao

○ Chungthang

Carry a packed lunch to the Yumthang valley - the 'Valley of Flowers' - as, if the weather holds out, you will enjoy spending the whole day here.

Chungthang-Lachung	21 km	Yumthang-Zadong	30 km
Lachung-Yumthang	24 km	Lachung-Mt. Katao	26 km

The accommodation at Lachung is a couple of notches up from that at Lachen so spending two nights here is quite easy. The day involves carrying a picnic lunch into the Yumthang valley, located at 12,000ft/3650m and an hour's scenic drive away. However, since the weather can deteriorate in the late afternoon, an 8 a.m. departure is recommended.

Your drive takes you through the Singhba Reserve Forest, otherwise called the 'Valley of Flowers of the East'. Rugged outcrops of polished brown sheer rock-face bring to mind the famous Dolomites of Italy and look even more striking as

they contrast the rich green trees lining your road.
Then start the rhodendron trees and bushes – a
riot of every conceivable colour and shade you
can imagine in rhododendrons! Set amid streams
and rocks these flowering bushes suggest the work
of a Great Master, creating a natural Zen garden
the best landscape artist couldn't hope to achieve!
In full bloom, the natural beauty of this valley
just completely overwhelms you and fills you with
awe at Nature's bountiful art.

Although you might never want that drive to
end, it does, 24km down the road in a beautiful
meadow of rolling green, often dotted with
peacefully grazing yaks and a small shop selling
hot drinks – as pastoral and peaceful as you
could hope for! The meadow slopes down to a
small crystal clear stream and is edged with rich
forests on the opposite bank, with snow peaks
looming in the background. There is a PWD Rest

Sheer rock face on the drive in to Yumthang valley

House and just before the meadows, off the road, are hot water springs. They originate behind the bathing hut and have been diverted into two pools for convenience.

If you have carried enough food and drink, you can spend as much time as you want, soaking in the beauty of the environment without the usual attendant hordes of tourists!

Once back and rested, you can walk around the town or visit the local monastery in the evening.

For the adventurous and experienced trekker, a start around 6 a.m. would take you to the road-head at Zadong, 30km ahead of Yumthang. A three-hour steep climb through snows brings you to the Donkiala Pass at 18,100ft/5500m where you have a panoramic view of the Tibetan plateau and the Cholamu Lake. Special permission and a guide familiar with the terrain are essential as are the usual trappings of high altitude trekking ■

Rhododendrons in full bloom in the Yumthang valley

◗◗ **Summit Mount Katao and return to Gangtok**

| Lachung-Mt. Katao | 26 km | Chungthang-Phodong | 55 km |
| Lachung-Chungthang | 21 km | Phodong-Gangtok | 40 km |

In case you plan to do some climbing, boots and parkas are available in Lachung to help you negotiate the snow.

The Lachung skyline is dominated by what appears to be a craggy giant – it is difficult to imagine that you can actually drive up to it and summit the adjoining Mt. Katao – or almost summit it, as the road ends 100m short of the top. The distance travelled is less than 30km and takes approximately an hour each way. Snow boots are available for hire and one can actually attempt the climb to the top and still be back in Lachung for lunch!!

Just out of Lachung are the Bhim and Bop waterfalls that are worth a short stop on your journey back to Gangtok. Another possible detour is Phodong, 40km before Gangtok and a kilometer uphill from the highway. There are two old monasteries here; Phodong, belonging to the Kagyupa sect, was built in the first quarter of the seventeenth century whereas Labrong, belonging to the Nyingmapa order, was built a hundred years later. Below the road to these two monasteries are the ruins of Tumlong, the third capital of Sikkim, later abandoned for Gangtok.

Relax and have a hot shower back in your hotel in Gangtok as the 'tough' part of your trip is over, and the next two to four days are to be spent in comparatively luxurious and laid-back surroundings. Sightseeing can be restricted to whatever you pick from the package of goodies available in the next few pages ■

Near the summit of Mt. Katao

⟫ From Gangtok to Pelling

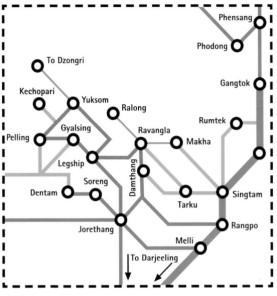

We recommend spending the night at Ravangla and if that is what you have planned, make a leisurely start.

Gangtok-Singtam	29 km	Legship-Gyalsing	15 km
Singtam-Melli	31 km	Gyalsing-Pelling	09 km
Melli-Jorethang	29 km	Singtam-Ravangla	36 km
Jorethang-Legship	25 km	Ravangla-Legship	26 km

The fastest route is by the national highway to Siliguri. At Melli, 60km from Gangtok, take the right turn onto the road to Jorethang (29km from Melli), then onto Legship which is 25km and finally to Pelling (24km). At Legship a short stop is called for to visit the Shiva temple, which is in an extremely picturesque location, on the banks of the Rangit River. The last 9km between Gyalsing (Geysing) and Pelling is a C-grade road and quite a rough ride. It is possible to avoid some of this hardship by ignoring the sign to Pelling that you will see at the T-junction and head right to Gyalsing and take the road past the police station

If you are pushing on to Pelling don't expect much in terms of food en route. However, there is an abundance of scenic spots to stop at and enjoy a packed lunch.

– a rather steep ascent but comparatively smoother till the last 3km. This route on the Siliguri highway is not as scenic as the alternate one and you duplicate a part of the journey taken while coming into Gangtok. The Pelling–Melli section is covered anyway when you are heading back.

However, if you decide to take this faster route,

The Teesta River

20km away from Gangtok is the Fambhong Lho Wildlife Sanctuary, which may be visited after obtaining the requisite permit from Gangtok. Spread over 5200 hectares, this sanctuary is home to the red panda, Himalayan black bear, civet cat and other species; you may get lucky and spot some wildlife!

The alternative route, which we would

recommend, involves turning off the national highway at Singtam (29km from Gangtok), onto Ravangla (36km), and Kewzing (10km) that has the only Bon monastery in Sikkim. Unlike many others, this monastery is very accessible as it is on the road and does not involve any climbing! If you are not pressed for time it is worth a quick 'dekho'.

You proceed to Legship, with the Shiva temple on the Rangit riverbank, and then on to Pelling (40km).

In terms of mileage, this route is actually a few kilometers shorter but takes thirty to forty-five

View of Mt. Narsing from Ravangla

minutes longer because it is more curvaceous. It is definitely far more scenic and cooler as most of the time you are coasting at an altitude above 4000ft/1200m. However, as mentioned earlier, the last 9km of the route is a C-grade road and the turn off towards Gyalsing town with the steep ascent on the narrower but smoother approach to Pelling is recommended.

Ravangla is a picturesque town lying on a ridge between Maenem Hill (10,600ft/3200m) and Tendong (8700ft/2650m), and affords magnificent views of Mount Narsing and the adjacent peaks.

If you are staying at the scenically perched Mt. Narsing Resort, remember the drive up is challenging and can be unnerving if attempted in the dark!

One of the four sacred caves lies just out of Ravangla, but despite the walk being pleasant the cave is a bit of a let down.

Ravangla is a good place to stop for lunch but if time permits, we recommend spending a night here as there are some interesting places to visit in the area and good accommodation available too.

During Pang Lhabsol, in August-September, this quiet township transforms to one of colour, gaiety and celebrations. Sikkim's guardian deity,

Kanchendzonga is worshipped and the Warrior Dance performed at the Mani Chokarling Monastery.

A little (8km or so), out of town on the road to Damthang, clear days offer a glorious view of the Singelila range – Pandim, Rathong, Kabur, Jopuno and Mt. Narsing are all clearly visible.

The long horns brought out for a prayer ceremony at Ralong Monastery

The Temi Tea Estate is 12km from Damthang and the only tea garden in Sikkim. The tea produced here is a rare blend of flavour and liquor found nowhere else and commands a high rate in the international markets.

Off the Damthang road, 6km from Ravangla, lies Tinkitam village which boasts a rare species of orchid, called the 'lady's slipper' that grows on the ground rather than on trees and flowers in October-November.

The Karma Rabtenling Monastery in Ralong (13km from the town center), is believed to have come up in 1768 at a spot where rice thrown from Tibet by the 9th Karmapa of the Kagyupa sect, fell. Pang Lhabsol celebrations and Kagyed masked dances are held here while the Mahakala dance is performed in November at the Palchen Choeling Monastic Institute. Palchen Choeling is a new monastery, built in 1995, and in appearance is a smaller replica of the one at Rumtek. There are hot sulphur springs below Ralong and Borong (10km from Ravangla). Reaching them involves a forty-five minute climb down to the Rangit River, and they are usable only between December and February most years, depending on the level of water in the river.

This route also offers an interesting variation if you have the inclination for a bit of walking.

From Singtam, you can drive to Tarku (16km), then on to Temi (8km) and Damthang (another 20km). From here there is a 2.5 hour climb on a bridle path through the dense forest of the Tendong Sanctuary. Tendong, at an altitude of around 8700ft/2650m, lies on a small plateau on top of the mountain. The view from here is breathtakingly awesome — it is akin to sitting in the middle of a huge amphitheatre and no other place in Sikkim offers such a panoramic view of

If it's a toss up between visiting the Ralong or the Bon monastery our vote is for the latter — it is the only one of its kind in Sikkim and the differences are very interesting.

Blossoms in October

the state's mountain range. On the East the entire Chola range is visible as is the Singelila with the towering Kanchendzonga in the West. Also visible are Darjeeling, Gangtok, Nathu La and the rolling plains around Siliguri. It is believed that this is the place where the Lepchas sought refuge when a great flood inundated the world — a story that finds parallels with that of Noah's Ark and Mt. Arafat.

Another beautiful trek is the 12km walk up to the Maenem peak through rich, sylvan forests of rhododendron, oak, chestnut and magnolia — the area is a declared sanctuary.

Off the main road from Gangtok and 7.5km from Ravangla is a village called Sangmo. Closeby here you can visit one of the Four Great Holy Caves of Sikkim — Sherchock Pephu, 'the secret cave of the East'. You have to take a 3km descending dirt track that is marked by a roadside sign for 'Primary Health Subcenter, Sangmo'. Look out for a faded red sign on the right hand side — from here it is a gentle twenty to twenty-five minute walk to the cave whose location is marked by prayer flags. However, the site has been neglected and the entrance is in a state of disrepair. Until the authorities improve things, this site is not recommended.

In this variation of the alternate route, if you are not interested in the treks, you can proceed to Pelling via one of two optional routes.

From Damthang, the journey to Pelling is 75km or two hours via Ravangla or 82km via Namchi and Jorethang. Namchi is worth a visit for those interested in seeing the recently built statue of Guru Padmasambhava which rises to 138ft and is located on the Samdruptse hill. This statue of the patron saint of Sikkim is the tallest statue of Guru Padmasambhava in the world ∎

Ravangla is an excellent choice for spending a couple of nights — you can just chill or get in a couple of good easy treks.

⏩ In and around Pelling

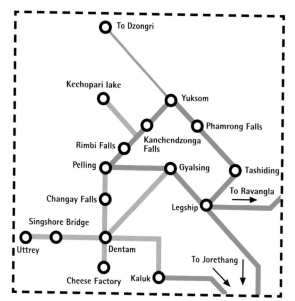

One or two early morning wake-ups are almost mandatory; there are only a few places where you can watch the big mountains light up from your bedroom window.

Pelling-Kechopari	27 km	Tashiding-Legship	13 km
Kechopari-Yuksom	28 km	Legship-Pelling	24 km
Yuksom-Tashiding	19 km	Pelling-Dentam	17 km

Pemayangtse Monastery, Rabdentse Palace Ruins, Sangochoeling Gompa, Changay Waterfall, Dentam Cheese Factory, Singshore Suspension Bridge, Kechopari Lake, Kanchendzonga Waterfall, Yuksom, Dubri Gompa, Phamrong Waterfall, and Tashiding Gompa.

PEMAYANGTSE MONASTERY

The monastery is only 2km from Pelling and is the most important monastery of the Nyingmapa order. It had humble origins as a small gompa built in the late seventeenth century. Around 1705, during the reign of the 3rd Chogyal, Chakdor Namgyal, it was rebuilt as a huge

The Pemayangtse Monastery near Pelling

monastery with a main hall covering 180 sq m. Standing at almost 7000ft/2150m, Pemayangtse (Perfect Sublime Lotus), is surrounded on two sides by snow-capped mountains.

The induction of monks to this monastery was restricted to those of pure Tibetan blood (celibate and 'pure', as in 'without deformities') and they were known as the Tu Song (Pure Monks). The head lama had the honour of anointing the

Walking up to the Pemayangtse Monastery knocks the breath out of you; you can drive up all the way and take a leisurely stroll in the forest while visiting the Rabdentse Palace.

Chogyal with holy water.

The exterior of this three-storey building is somewhat plain but has been embellished with the addition of a new gate inaugurated with much fanfare in 2003. The interior is extremely ornate with a prominent image of Guru Padmasambhava framed by a wood carving of serpents entwined around a staff. There is a gruesome image of Dorje Phurba and a more pleasant one of Chenresig. On

the top floor is the Zandong Palri, the seven-tiered heavenly abode of Guru Padmasambhava, complete with rainbows, angels and the whole panoply of Buddhas and Boddhisattavas. This was built single-handed by Dungzin Rinpoche and the task took five years! The main chaam, or dance, is held in February each year on the last days of the 12th Tibetan lunar month.

THE RABDENTSE PALACE RUINS
A half hour walk through a thick forest will take you to the scattered ruins of the Rabdentse Palace. This second capital of Sikkim was established in 1670 and later abandoned because of proximity to

If you make it to Dentam and visit the cheese factory you could get up to 15% off on your purchases.

the Nepalese border from where there were frequent raids. The chortens around the palace have survived the ravages of time and the complex has now been taken over by the Archeological Survey of India and declared a protected monument. With the snow mountains in the background this is a site to be visited.

THE SANGOCHOELING GOMPA

The Sangochoeling Gompa (Land of the Sacred Spell) is a 45-minute (2.5km) uphill walk from the Pelling football field. Built in 1697 this is the oldest gompa to have been built in Sikkim. The original was destroyed in an earthquake hence the

Chortens at the Rabdentse Palace

Sangochoeling Gompa, above Pelling

current structure is a more recent construction. Unlike the Pemayangtse Monastery, the admittance policy was more egalitarian and was open to all classes and races; it was one of the few gompas that admitted women as nuns. Belonging to the Nyingmapa order, Sangochoeling houses fine images of Lord Buddha and Guru Padmasambhava – the wall paintings are muted but the sculptures are quite ostentatious. A new road is under construction and soon this peaceful and hitherto remote gompa, set in a rich verdant forest, will become all too easily accessible.

THE CHANGAY WATERFALL

This waterfall lies 10km from Pelling on the road to Dentam and is definitely worth a visit. A little further (10km), is the Sikkim Alpine cheese factory set up with a Swiss collaborator. Worth a visit if you want to see the manufacturing process and pick up some of their delicious cheese (advisable to be there before 2 p.m). Have a wholesome well-cooked meal at Surya Hotel owned by Karuna in the main market; (meal for three washed down with a bottle of Dansberg beer for just Rs.110!). The 198m long Singshore

Tantric wall paintings inside the gompa

The Singshore Suspension Bridge suspension bridge cuts a rather dramatic picture and can be reached 4km from Dentam, on the road to Uttaray (5km beyond the bridge and on the border with Nepal).

KECHOPARI LAKE

The next day's visit to Kechopari (Wishing) Lake involves a bit of driving as it is 27km from Pelling. En route lies the Rimbi waterfall – it is only 12km out of Pelling but not particularly inspiring or worthy of a halt. The Kechopari Lake (6400ft/1950m), is considered to be sacred and lies in a small shallow valley surrounded by densely forested hills. Seen aerially, the lake resembles a giant foot. This is believed to be a footprint of Guru Padmasambhava, which is probably one of the reasons for its 'holy' status. Prayer flags adorn the shore and there is a wooden walkway to the water's edge with colourful prayer wheels flanking the sides. Local lore holds that the lake's surface stays amazingly clear of fallen, floating leaves no matter what the time of year, day or night or even in stormy weather — we certainly didn't spot any on both our visits! Apparently birds from the surrounding forest have been entrusted with the responsibility of keeping the holy lake clean and pure. Though it looks tempting, swimming is a strict no-no, but a cup of coffee at the dhaba near the entrance is recommended.

The place for wishes and prayers — Kechopari, the 'wishing' Lake

Pelling offers brilliant snow views but if you do not want to spend all your time there, Yuksom is a good alternative - it is very pleasant destination though the views are not as great.

YUKSOM

From Kechopari Lake it is a short 28km drive to Yuksom. En route one crosses a quaint suspension bridge over the Rutang Chu. The majestic Kanchendzonga waterfall, 9km before Yuksom is a fantastic place to stop for a drink or even a lunch break, and at certain times in the year when the rush of water is less, you can scramble over the rocks and get behind the fall's water curtain! If still inclined for a swim, this is a great place to

On the climb up to Tashiding

take a dip. The pool at the waterfall's base, although cold is very refreshing.

From here the road climbs to Yuksom, which affords good views of the North and South peaks of Kabru. This was the first capital of Sikkim and the spot where the three holy men met is tucked away in a quiet corner midst a grove of trees. The original stone throne marks the spot where the actual coronation took place and there is a footprint on an adjacent rock face, said to be that of Lama Lhatsun Chembo, formed in the seventeenth century.

The Dubdi Gompa, built by Lhatsun Chembo in 1701, if not the first is certainly one of Sikkim's oldest gompas. It lies above Yuksom along a steep path that takes around forty minutes to traverse. Monks are no longer in residence here and unless the caretaker, who resides in the village, accompanies you it will not be possible to enter or view the images of Guru Padmasambhava, Chenresig and the first Chogyal that lie inside.

From Yuksom you could either return to Pelling or proceed to Tashiding Gompa, reputedly the most sacred in Sikkim. Keep in mind that though the onward drive is only 19km, the return via Legship is a long 40km one. Visiting the gompa, also involves a forty-five minute uphill walk and we recommend covering this the next day. However, if you do carry on, we suggest seeing the Phamrong waterfall from the road – although quite a remarkable series of falls when viewed from further up, the path to the viewpoint is badly damaged by landslips.

The mani walls located at the extreme end of the Tashiding complex are one of its most fascinating features. Look out for the master artisan at work, chipping and etching the stones with diligence and reverence.

TASHIDING GOMPA

This gompa is the most sacred in Sikkim, the mere sight of which is supposed to cleanse you of your sins! It lies on top of a hill rising between the Rathong and Rangit rivers, "at the end of a rainbow that emanated from Mt. Kanchendzonga". The beautiful gompa is set on a plateau above the village and has a commanding view. It is surrounded by hundreds of prayer flags that resemble an army awaiting orders to march! Originally built in 1716, this gompa belongs to the Nyingmapa order and was extensively renovated and expanded during the reign of the third Chogyal. The current building was established in

1987 when the original gompa was dismantled, but six of the eight original pillars have been used in the new building. The main prayer hall has an image of Buddha flanked by four Boddhisattavas on each side. There is also a veritable forest of chortens in the adjoining enclosure – these numerous chortens are dedicated to various Chogyals and other religious leaders. They are enclosed by a 'mani' wall with the prayer stones skilfully and intricately carved with Buddha images and the Buddhist mantra "Om Mane Padme Hum".

Particularly interesting is this gompa's role in auguring the future of the state. During the annual Bhumchu festival, celebrated in March, water from a sacred vase (Bhumpa) is mixed with

Tashiding Gompa

Resembling an army on the move... prayer flags at Tashiding

water from the Rathong and Rangit rivers and distributed to devotees by the head lama of Tashiding. The bowl is then refilled and locked away for one year. When it is taken out for the next year's Bhumchu, the lama makes prognostications according to the amount of water still contained in the vessel. A low level of water is a sign of ill tidings, heralding disease, poor harvest, drought or famine; if the vessel is full to the brim, there will be bloodshed in Sikkim, but if the vessel is half full, there will be an abundant crop and peace will reign in Sikkim.

We recommend this as an excursion for your third day, but if time is short, the climb to Dubdi Gompa can be avoided and instead Kechopari Lake, Yuksom and Tashiding can be covered in a day ■

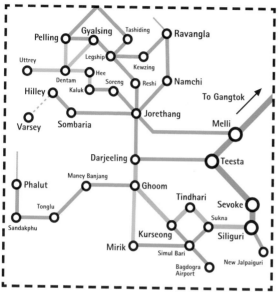

In case you have missed lunch in Siliguri do not despair! The chicken cutlets at the airport restaurant are pretty good!

Pelling-Legship	24 km	Hilley-Jorethang	55 km
Legship-Jorethang	25 km	Jorethang-Darjeeling	38 km
Jorethang-Melli	29 km	Darjeeling-Siliguri	78 km
Melli-Siliguri	54 km		

Allow for a three to four hour drive to Siliguri with a possible half hour diversion to visit the Kandosanphug (Cave of Fairies), located near the hot springs of Reshi which you pass on your way down. If you want to end on a wet but happy note, factor in two to three hours of rafting on the Teesta.

A hot lunch at Siliguri after this would be ideal and the chicken curry and chicken cutlets at the airport restaurant are recommended. However, if you are fond of seafood, you must definitely check out 'Kalpatru Pice', a well reputed local dhaba on Sevoke Road in Siliguri. The place itself is quite shabby but the food is outstanding –

Bamboo by the road, between Siliguri and Kurseong

specially recommended are the Aar, Ilish (Hilsa) and Jhinga (Prawns) – non-fishy items are very much part of the 100 dish menu! For those of you planning to include a visit to Darjeeling – on its own or along with Kalimpong – the route is common upto Jorethang. From here instead of turning left and crossing the river, proceed straight on. A twisting, steeply ascending road with a bad surface brings you to Darjeeling. Though the distance is less than 30km, allow two hours for this journey.

DARJEELING

The widely accepted version on the origin of the name, Darjeeling, is that it was actually called 'Dorje-ling', meaning 'place of the thunderbolt'. This is believed to be the place where God Indra's sceptre (thunderbolt) rested and the word is also an allusion to the intense pre-monsoon storms that frequent the area. However, some believe that the name derives from Lama Dorje Rinzing who meditated and had his gompa atop Observatory Hill. Though the shrine was subsequently shifted to the Bhutia Bustee Gompa, the area retained the name of 'the place of Dorje Lama'.

You are back in the thick of civilization in Darjeeling. Be prepared for traffic jams and 'no parking' zones.

Darjeeling, (pop. 75,000), enjoys a commanding location at a height of 7000ft/2134m. The British discovered this vast tract of mountainous, densely forested, uninhabited land in 1829 during a military expedition led by Gen. Lloyd against the marauding Gorkha army. The possibility of establishing a sanatorium at this strategic location, the doorway to Sikkim, Nepal and Bhutan, struck J.W. Grant (Commercial Resident, Malda), and by means more foul than fair the land was wrested from the Sikkim Chogyal. In 1839, Darjeeling got its first superintendent–the famous Dr. Campbell and by 1863 seventy homes had been built in the best British tradition. Daunting as the task was, a road from Pankhabari was hewed out of the dense jungle and this access enabled the establishment of tea plantations. There was now no looking back now! In a feat of engineering ingenuity, the Darjeeling Himalayan Railway Company linked this remote area with Siliguri in only two years, working under the most difficult conditions sans any modern construction equipment. Our bureaucratic rulers today certainly need to take a page or two out of history while planning and implementing their grandiose projects!

Darjeeling is only 80km away from Siliguri,

Darjeeling has a great choice of restaurants with good food. We recommend Taaja's and Glenarys, both of which are centrally located. For a meal served with style, head to the lofty heights, of Windamere Hotel. Carrying this book may even get you discounts!

View from Tiger Hill

which is the base station for all road travel to Sikkim, Bhutan, Darjeeling and Kalimpong. However, barring the first twenty odd kilometers that are flat and the road surface relatively smooth, the rest of the journey is a veritable nightmare. This is probably the worst of all roads connecting a major hill destination in our country. The Pankhabari route from the airport is shorter by 15km but involves a series of steep switchbacks with monumental craters threatening to swallow your tyres, just as you take the turn! Unlike other hill routes, the youngsters driving taxis downhill here do not believe in giving those struggling up the customary right of way.

TREKS

Darjeeling is the base for treks to Sandakhphu (59km towards the North-East at an altitude of 11,950ft/3640m) and Phalut (11,600ft/3540m) which lies 22km further, on the Singelila ridge. Views of Kanchendzonga and the North face of Everest are particularly good, as also Cholamari the highest peak of Bhutan. (Both these points are accessible by jeep though the track is rough and the 80km journey takes upto 6 hours each way) Phalut lies at the tri-junction of Nepal, Sikkim and West Bengal and a 4km trek takes one to Singelila (12,100ft/3686m). Another 4km brings one down to the Chiwabhan-jang pass which leads to Nepal. From here one can trek onto the HMI base camp or descend to Varsey (4 hours).

We would recommend adding an additional 20km to your journey and taking the road to Mirik Lake that is at a cool 5800ft/1767m. The turn-off is just before the steep ascent to Makaibari begins and this route is far less travelled. Mirik is a pleasant destination for lunch or even a night, if you are not pressed for time. Besides the undulating green carpet the tea

The famous Darjeeling tea....

gardens simulate, Mirik is known for its orange orchards which fruit from end October till January. It also offers good snow views and some very pleasant walks. This road connects with the Pankhabari road near Ghoom.

If this diversion is not appealing, and you are interested in learning what the world famous Darjeeling tea is all about, take on the challenge

Check out the Planters Club. The history is fascinating and it still retains an aura of its colonial past when the hardworking sahibs of the tea estates rode into town for a night out!

of the Pankhabari road but stop at the Makaibari Tea Estate located just short of the large town of Kurseong. This garden boasts of producing the most expensive tea in the world—a record breaking Rs.18,000 per kilo! They are one of the pioneers of organic tea, and also offer accommodation in an eco-camp on the estate. Owned and run by Rajah and Srirupa Banerjee, the estate is worth a quick 'dekho'. (Contact: Tel: 03594-2330181, 2330179; Website: www.makaibari.com e-mail: srirupa@sancharnet.in)

If you are driving down to Siliguri, you need to keep a sharp set of wits around you — it is almost a 'learner's track' where you are under constant attack! Some of the young drivers haven't got their act together and tend to be bullies on the road.

The 'main road' to Darjeeling starts from Siliguri town and meets up with the Pankhabari road at Kurseong. The climb is gentler, and if you don't plan to visit either of the two M's, (Makaibari or Mirik), this route rates a little better, but still not so great!

From Kurseong (which has little to recommend itself barring chicken cutlets at the Tourist Bungalow!) one passes through the pretty village of Tung with its multi-coloured, quaint houses. The hillsides are draped with enormous ferns and black cardamom (badi elaichi) plants and further

The Senchal Sanctuary

up a multitude of silken streams make their way through rich, mixed forests. Barring the road conditions, this drive is enjoyably scenic all the way to the high point at Ghoom (7410ft/2260m). From here it is a 6km descent to Darjeeling.

Today Darjeeling is an urban concrete jungle and has all the attendant problems associated with basic infrastructure being stretched to the limit and its subsequent breakdown. The summer and October 'puja break' bring in hoards of tourists and besides the over crowding, there is inevitably an acute water shortage. Add to this the din of blaring horns, engines straining up steep roads, pollution levels to rival any of our big cities and you certainly do not have the makings of a good, peaceful holiday!

The toy train stops for a break at the War Memorial near Ghoom

However, inspite of this chaos during the 'season', there are certain attractions inherent to the place that even we have not been able to ruin! Foremost is the setting which offers magnificent views of Mt. Kanchendzonga and the surrounding peaks. The largely vehicle-free Mall and Chowrasta areas are a pleasure to stroll through and unlike many other hill stations, Darjeeling has a reasonably active and buzzing night life (not very late though!). There are also a few good excursions out of town that can transport you to peaceful, sylvan surroundings in less than an hour. A limited period of stay is recommended in this erstwhile eastern 'Queen of the Hills', especially if you are visiting in high season.

Assuming you have scheduled a stay of two or

A ride on the 'Toy Train' to Ghoom is certainly a worthwhile experience though the tickets are a bit pricey at Rs. 250 per head.

Feel the spirit of the adventurers who led early expeditions to Mt. Everest and other peaks, while you view the exhibits at the Himalayan Institute of Mountaineering.

three days, the sights to be seen in town are few and easily done. The town is home to the famous Himalayan Institute of Mountaineering where exhibits of various expeditions to Mt. Everest and other peaks are on display; adjacent to this is the Padmaja Naidu Zoo, which is one of the few places in the world where the greatly endangered snow leopard has been successfully bred in captivity. Close by is the Lloyd Botanical Garden that derives its name from the illustrious William Lloyd, founder and owner of that very British institution –Lloyd's Bank. In 1879 he gifted forty

St. Andrew's Church in Darjeeling

acres of rolling hillside to be converted into one of Asia's best gardens. A brilliant array of azaleas, geraniums, orchids, arum lilies and many other flowers combine with a verdant tropical forest, with its own multitude of species, to make this well planned garden worth a visit.

While walking on the Mall you cannot fail to notice and admire St. Andrew's Church. The climb up to the top of Observatory Hill is somewhat steep, but a visit to the Mahakal Temple and the original Buddhist shrine of Lama Dorje Rinzing makes you glad you made the effort. Gaily

Bangle offerings at a temple en route to Tiger Hill

decorated with prayer flags this spot is venerated by both the Buddhist and Hindu communities. The Hindu temple surrounded by Buddhist prayer flags is testimony to the harmony and intermingling of the two religions in this area.

From here one can visit the Bhutia Bustee Gompa with its lovely snow views. Rebuilt by the Sikkim Chogyal after the 1934 earthquake, the monks here are part of the Red Hat sect and their library houses the original copy of The Tibetan Book of The Dead – the *'Bhando Thandol'*.

A visit to the Planters Club, overlooking the start of the main Mall, should be part of your Darjeeling experience as it has seen some glorious and interesting times, being the most popular watering hole for the British tea planters of yore. A few original Snaffles paintings, depicting the colonial era, adorn the walls of the lounge while two old oxygen cylinders by the entrance are remnants of the ill fated expedition to Mt. Everest led by Irvine & Mallory, that started here in 1924 and ended so tragically. The 'Quarter Deck' has a Maxim Nordenfelt machine gun used by Col. Younghusband during his expedition to Tibet in 1905 and the billiards room has photographs of the third Everest expedition, as also various trophies won in polo and racing competitions.

You could continue this journey through time by taking a ride on the 'Toy' train that has a special run for tourists from Darjeeeling to Ghoom and back. This narrow gauge train began in 1881 and covered 88km from New Jalpaiguri to Darjeeling and is now a UNESCO World Heritage project. The original Boyennold steam engines have completed a century and the entire journey undertakes a remarkable climb from near sea level to a height of 7410ft/2,260m. With its puffing steam engine, the two-hour return trip includes a stop at the Gorkha War Memorial at the Batasia loop and a visit to the railway museum at Ghoom. Although a little expensive, the ride is a delightful and unique experience.

The Dirdhan Temple, modelled on the famous Pashupatinath Temple in Kathmandu, lies just below the railway station and is possibly the most important Hindu temple of the area.

A visit to Tiger Hill is a must as the views from here are unparalleled. It is 1000 ft higher than Darjeeling and although only 11km away, the drive could take as much as thirty minutes during the tourist season. Everyone heads to the top of the hill, with its ugly concrete viewing center, that has a more expensive upper section enclosed in glass as a protection from the cold. However, just short of the hilltop is a grassy ridge, running

Both Darjeeling and Kalimpong have well-stocked nurseries that carry a beautiful array of plants and flowers. You can buy some to carry back or arrange to have them sent to your home.

Darjeeling is quite the happening place in the evenings! Buzz at Glenarys has live music most nights and Joey's Bar is a lively hang out. The Mayfair and Elgin hotels also have plush watering holes.

along the road, which offers brilliant views of the sunrise over Mt. Kanchendzonga without having to jostle for vantage space. There is also a track leading up to the burnt shell of a tourist bungalow that was destroyed in the 1980s, when the Gorkhaland agitation ignited more than passions. Apparently the undulating 'greens' adjoining this bungalow were once a demanding nine-hole golf course and this is yet another great spot to watch the spectacular drama of the sun's first rays softly lighting up the range. In summer the 'show' starts just after 4.30 a.m. and though this means getting up really early, on a clear day

Outside the Yigachoeling
Gompa near Ghoom

the effort is well worth making.

The temple at the check-point to the hilltop is especially interesting as devotees have strung up thousands of red bangles as offerings.

For those interested in spending the day out in peaceful surroundings and amidst a verdant forest, a picnic outing to the adjacent Senchal Wildlife Sanctuary is strongly recommended. Located just a kilometer away from the base of the climb to Tiger Hill, the three artificial lakes located here are the source of Darjeeling's water. Entry to the sanctuary is by a permit obtainable from the Forest Office located at the end of Jorebungalow

township, on a track leading down from the main road and clearly marked by a large signboard. After getting the permit, head back for 50m to the Emmanuel Church and then take the track opposite, going up the hillside. From here it is less than 2km to the not-very-attractive Sindhap Lake. Around 800m further, look out for a dirt track leading up – this brings you to the twin Senchal lakes, whose beauty is somewhat marred by the

The man-made lakes in the Senchal Sanctuary are not particularly inspiring – less so when we were told the wire fencing was to thwart potential suicides! However, the drive in the forest is absolutely wonderful and of course a great way to escape from the city crowds.

surrounding wire mesh fence (we were told these had been installed to prevent suicides!). The main track continues through almost three kilometers of rich forest with gurgling streams and you feel perfectly in sync with nature, driving or walking to whichever idyllic spot you choose for a picnic. This is not really on the tourist map and you may have the place all to yourselves, the peace and quiet enhancing the atmosphere.

Senchal Lake

On the return journey, a 1.5km diversion from Ghoom takes you the Yigachoeling Monastery that is the oldest in the area. Built in 1875, its monks belong to the Gelugpa order. The image of the Maitreya is somewhat unusual; He is shown with blue eyes and seated, western style, with his hands on his knees. This is probably due to the belief that the next Buddha will manifest in the West and hence this image's rather unique depiction. You can also visit the Samdenchoeling Monastery, on the main road just outside Ghoom. A recent addition is the gigantic white Peace Pagoda, around 2km from Chowrasta. Rising almost 100ft this is one of a series of stupas set up to promote Buddhism and peace in the world.

Driving out of Darjeeling, we suggest you follow

Thangsa Gompa, Kalimpong

the scenic 36km (1.5hrs) road that lies on a ridge above the Teesta and offers great views of the river as it flows along the main highway to Gangtok. From here it is 14km to Kalimpong, or 60km (2hrs) to Gangtok. If you are headed for Pelling, in West Sikkim, there is a sharply descending narrow, rough road through tea gardens to Jorethang, which is only 38km away. Allow for two hours to cover this section. From here on you are on a good road up to Gyalsing via Legship (37km) and you should be able to this in about an hour. This is followed by the very bad 9km stretch to Pelling. (As suggested earlier you could reduce this bone-rattling experience by taking the better road to Gyalsing and then the steep road to Pelling, past the police station).

For Land Rover enthusiasts, Darjeeling is the real Mecca for vintage vehicles. This is the only place in the country where Land Rovers outnumber all other jeeps — they are used as taxis but even double as milk vans and general utility vehicles!

KALIMPONG

Kalimpong with a population of 50,000 is a smaller, less built-up version of Darjeeling. With the main town at 4000ft the highest point in town is Darpin hill (4598ft/1402m) Originally part of Sikkim, Kalimpong came under control of Bhutan in 1705 and then was ceded to the British in 1865. Till the war with China in 1962, it was an important trading center between India and Tibet with mule trains passing over the Jelepla pass and using the all weather Kalimpong-Jelepla road. In the latter part of the nineteenth century it became a center for Scottish missionary activity and was famed for the exemplary 'Dr. Graham's Home', a school set up for the 'less-privileged' progeny of the tea planters. Situated at the base of Deolo hill (which houses the three water reservoirs of the town), it has a chapel, dated 1925, with fine stained glass windows. The school is spread over 500 acres of rolling hillside and is now open to students from all backgrounds, with a quota for the disadvantaged. Visitors are welcome to visit the distinguished 100-year old buildings and buy fresh fruit, vegetables and other products of the school, from a shop near the entrance – in fact, as anyone from Kolkata will confirm, the cheese and chocolate lollipops from here have been famous for years!

There are a couple of gompas worth a quick visit—the oldest being the Bhutanese Thangsa Gompa, originally founded in 1692 but rebuilt after it was destroyed by the Gorkhas, just before the advent of the British. A recent addition is the Zong Palri Monastery, just below the crest of Darpin hill.

Darpin hill provides excellent views of the Chola range in Sikkim as well as of the Jelepla pass leading into Tibet while the North West horizon is

Kalimpong is much quieter than Darjeeling. The 'other Karmapa' is based here and with the right contacts, you can arrange a meeting with him.

dominated by the Kanchendzonga range. The
Deolo hilltop, at 5150ft/1570m, is another location
with brilliant snow views and ideal for picnics.

Dr. Graham's residence
in Kalimpong

  Kalimpong may be a bit of a disappointment as
a hill station since it neither offers any great
countryside walks off the tarmac, nor does it have
a particularly interesting evening life that was
evident. However, if you are looking for a longer
stay, in a moderate climate, this is a good place to
come to. For those with green fingers, the flora is
varied and beautiful and there are several
excellent nurseries ■

Suggested Itineraries and Cost

ITINERARIES

SHORT 'N' SPECTACULAR

DAYS

01	Arrive in Rumtek	Night at Rumtek
02	Rumtek Monastery & Gangtok local sights	Night at Gangtok
03	Tsomgo Lake, Nathu La, & Menmecho Lake	Night at Gangtok
04	Gangtok local sightseeing	Night at Gangtok
05	Drive to Lachung	Night at Lachung
06	Visit Yumthang - Valley of Flowers	Night at Lachung
07	Summit Mt. Katao	Night at Gangtok
08	Morning River Rafting	Night at home!

SHORT, WITH LUXURY ALL THE WAY!

01	Arrive in Rumtek	Night at Rumtek
02	Rumtek and Gangtok sightseeing	Night at Gangtok
03	Tsomgo Lake, Nathu La, and Menmecho Lake	Night at Gangtok
04	Drive to Pelling via Ravangla	Night at Pelling
05-7	Around Pelling	Night at Pelling
08	Rafting	Night at home!

SHORT, BUT COVERING A LOT OF GROUND

01	Arrive in Rumtek	Night at Rumtek
02	Rumtek Monastery & Gangtok sightseeing	Night at Gangtok
03	Visit Tsomgo Lake, Nathu La & Menmecho Lake	Night at Gangtok
04	Travel to Lachen or Lachung	Night at either
05	Gurudongmar Lake or Yumthang	Night at Lachung
06	Yumthang or Mt. Katao	Night at Lachung/ Gangtok
07	Mt Katao or Pelling	Night at Gangtok/Pelling
08	Rafting or Pelling	Night at Home/ Pelling
09	Rafting	Night at home!

THE FULL MONTY

01	Rumtek	Night at Rumtek
02	Rumtek and around	-do-
03	Gangtok sightseeing	Night at Gangtok
04	Nathu La, Menmecho and Tsomgo Lake	-do-
05	Drive to Lachen	Night at Lachen
06	Gurudongmar Lake	Night at Lachung
07	Yumthang	-do-

08	Mt. Katao	Night at Gangtok
09	Ravangla	Night at Ravangla
10	To Pelling via Tashiding	Night at Pelling
11	Pelling	-do-
12	Pelling	-do-
13	Pelling	-do-
14	Darjeeling	Night at Darjeeling
15	Darjeeling	-do-
16	Kalimpong	Night at Kalimpong
17	Rafting	Night at home!

LUXURY ALL THE WAY!

01	Rumtek	Night at Rumtek
02	Rumtek	-do-
03	Gangtok	Night at Gangtok
04	Nathu La, Menmecho & Tsongmo Lakes	-do-
05	Gangtok	-do-
06	Ravangla	Night at Ravangla
07-10	Pelling & around	Nights at Pelling
11-13	Darjeeling*	Nights at Darjeeling
14-15	Kalimpong	Nights at Kalimpong
16	Rafting	Night at home!

MIX 'N' MATCH

01 & 2	Rumtek	Nights at Rumtek
03 & 4	Gangtok	Nights at Gangtok
05 & 6	Lachung	Nights at Lachung
07	Gangtok	Night at Gangtok
08	Ravangla	Night at Ravangla
09-12	Pelling	Nights at Pelling
13	Rafting and return or proceed to Darjeeling and follow the 'luxury' itinerary	

* If it is rhododendron flowering season visit Varsey for the day. You can also spend the night, but it involves a 4km walk from the road head at Hilley. If one leaves Pelling early, you can have a picnic lunch and reach Darjeeling in the evening. Please note that the road from Jorethang upto Darjeeling is bad and should be negotiated while it is still light.

TRIP COSTS

We have made an attempt to provide an estimate costing for a 12-day holiday for a couple, with the journey starting and ending at Siliguri.

	BEST HOTELS	MEDIUM	BUDGET
Stay	Rs. 25000	Rs. 12000	Rs. 8000
Food	Rs. 8000	Rs. 5000	Rs. 4000
Transport*	Rs. 30000	Rs. 25000	Rs. 25000
River Rafting	Rs. 2000	Rs. 1500	Rs. 1500

* If you are 4 or 6 people there can be considerable savings on this head

HOW TO GET THERE

BY AIR

FROM DELHI
Daily flights at around 10 a.m. to Bagdogra (approx 2 hrs. flying time) Return flights at around 2 p.m.

MUMBAI
Morning flight to Delhi or Kolkata to take connecting flight to Bagdogra.

KOLKATA
Daily flights at around 10 a.m. to Bagdogra Return flights around noon.

BANGALORE
Morning flight to Kolkata. Connecting flight to Bagdogra. Evening return flight from Kolkata.

CHENNAI
Evening flight to Kolkata. Overnight stay. Morning flight to Bagdogra Evening flight back to Chennai.

BY RAIL

FROM DELHI
By Guwahati Rajdhani. Dep 1715 hrs. Arr. New Jalpaiguri 1410 hrs. Return departure at 1240 hrs Arrival in Delhi 1010 hrs.

KOLKATA
There are four trains which leave between 1500 hrs and 2100 hrs, reaching New Jalpaiguri the next morning. Return to Kolkata, departures between 1500 and 2000 hrs.

TREKKING AND RAFTING

TREKKING IN SIKKIM

From the lush sylvan terrain of the more temperate South to the beautiful panoramas in the East, the breathtaking wilderness in the North to the magnificent snow peaks in the West, Sikkim has an incredible bounty of natural beauty to offer. It is truly a trekker's paradise!

However, having relied more on his trusty four wheelers than his two legs, the author has little experience in anything more strenuous than a three to four hour trek!! The information in this section is, therefore, not based on first hand experiences but an effort has been made to segregate treks by geographical location, and within that, in order of difficulty.

TREKKING SEASON

MARCH–MAY AND SEPTEMBER–NOVEMBER
Trekking above 13,500ft/4100m is not advised till April as many regions are still covered with snow, making the route difficult to discern and negotiate.

Setting off for a trek

WALKS & TREKS

FROM GANGTOK ▶▶ From the Tashi
View Point to Tinjure, on the top of
the hill opposite Gangtok, is a day's
easy trek. This takes one through the
thick forest of the Fambhong Lho
Wildlife Sanctuary to the highest
point where there is a three-storied
Observation Tower. The views of
Tendong peak and Mt. Siniolchu are

Heading into the clouds

breathtaking and the trek is approximately 8km each way.

FROM RAVANGLA ▶▶ The Sherchock
Pephu (Secret Cave), which is one of
the Four Great Holy Caves, can be
reached by walking to Sangmo,
(5km from Ravangla), and then descending for around thirty minutes.

After a short (20km) drive to
Damthang you can walk through the
Tendong forest to ascend the
Tendong hill, which involves a climb

of close to 2000ft/600m over a distance of 5km. For descriptions of this area, read the section on Ravangla and the drive from Gangtok to Pelling.

A more strenuous trek is the one to the Maenem hilltop, which involves a climb of 4000ft/1200m covering a distance of 10km. A further walk of 2km takes you to Bhaley Dunga, a cliff top shaped like a rooster's head and visible from afar. The journey takes approximately four hours each way.

Borong is a picturesque village facing the snow-capped peaks and is home to the Tsa-chu or sulphur hot springs famed for their medicinal properties. This is a four hour trek, but is also accessible by road.

A five to six day trek originates at Damthang and covers Tendong, Maenem, Ravangla & Borong. Tendong hill, covered in rich forest is used by many a Buddhist monk for meditation and retreat, and carries an aura of solitude and grandeur. The Maenem Sanctuary is home to the red panda, Himalayan black bear, assorted deer and a fantastic variety of birds. It has a thick cover of oaks, chestnut and rhododendron and unparalleled views of Kanchendzonga.

FROM YUKSOM ▶▶ This is where the first Chogyal was crowned and the stone throne and altar is to be found in a peaceful spot surrounded by trees. Yuksom is one of the most frequented starting point for trekkers and is well equipped for their needs. Some of the popular routes are:

Yuksom-Zongri to Kanchendzonga Base Camp is a 26km trek. Starting at 5800ft/1750m, you walk on relatively flat land for an hour and then climb to Bakhim, 14km away at 9000ft/2740m, along a tree-lined path. There is a Forest Bungalow here or you could proceed on to Tsokha, at 9700ft/2950m a few kilometers up, where there is a trekker's hut and private lodge. Tsokha to Zongri, at 13,300ft/4000m, is through rhododendron trees and overlooking spectacular views of Pandim, Narsing and Kanchendzonga peaks. There is a camping ground here as well as trekker's huts and another hour and half can take you to Zongri La, the pass from which the entire Kanchendzonga range is visible.

From Zongri there is a 10km trek to the Himalayan Mountaineering Institute base camp located at 15,000ft/4600m.

Another route from Zongri takes one on a 14km trek to the Goech La pass at 16,200ft/4950m, with accommodation being available at Zemathang, 4km before the pass.

Base Camp and onto The Lakes, is a four to five day round trip via Botak to Laxmipokhari with the return via

Gerakhet. En route one encounters six to eight high altitude lakes – the trek is at an average altitude of 13,500ft/4100m and is one of the most beautiful and less frequented trails.

HIGH ALTITUDE TREKS IN NORTH SIKKIM

Lachen to Green Lake is a 32km trek, starting at 9000ft/2700m on the Lachen-Thangu road, past the confluence of the Zemu and Lachen rivers, along Zemu Chu, up to Jakthang at 10,800ft/3300m, where trekker's huts provide basic facilities. From Jakthang, you climb to Yabuk, which is the mouth of the Zemu glacier. You then follow the glacier and climb up to Sona Camp at 14,750ft/4500m from where you have an unobstructed view of the beautiful needlepoint Siniolchu peak. Almost the entire trek from here to the Green Lake, at 16,000ft/4850m, affords brilliant views of some of the most imposing peaks in the Himalayan range. The trek takes three days each way.

Another trek starts from Thangu and involves a grueling 9km climb to Muguthang. From here one can reach the Green Lake (15km away) or go upto the Chortenyimala pass, which leads into Tibet and lies 18km from Muguthang.

Trekking requires special permits, which can be organised by your tour operator.

RAFTING

Rafting is possible on both the Teesta as well as the Rangit, but rafting on the latter is generally restricted to the period after the monsoon since the water level is then well above the treacherous rocks. The starting point on the Rangit is Sikip (before Jorethang) and the adventurous ride ends at Melli.

The Teesta offers a placid, beginner's stretch from Melli down to the Coronation bridge and a more exhilarating four and a half hour roller coaster involving Grade II and III+ rapids, from Bordang to Melli. This is a wonderful way to end your holiday and it is possible to raft on the Teesta between October and May. Take your pick of the gentle or slightly more exciting stretch. Remember that you are more than likely to get wet and hence keep a change ready before you head onto the airport or railway station for your homeward journey. Unlike other parts of the country, rafting in Sikkim is still in its infancy. It is important that you select an operator who has received adequate training and has good equipment.

A series of hydro-electric projects are at the advanced planning stage and if implemented rafting on the Teesta will be a thing of the past.

HELICOPTER SIGHTSEEING

Sikkim tourism has organised short duration (twenty minutes to seventy minutes) flights for groups of five people at a time. Covering Gangtok, and North and West Sikkim the cost is between Rs.3000 and 5000 per person for each excursion ▪

AUTHOR'S NOTE

Within these treks there are also some shorter 2-3 day options available. If you specify what you want to do, your tour guide can tailor-make a trekking itinerary to suit your preferences.

Rafting down the Teesta

THE ENVIRONMENT AND YOU

*"Take nothing but pictures,
kill nothing but time,
leave nothing but footprints".*

THE importance of respecting, preserving and not polluting the environment wherever we travel cannot be over-emphasised. Whenever we travel overseas we marvel at the cleanliness, the lack of litter, the absence of plastic, foil, wrappers and so on. Yet within our own environ many travellers treat the roads, pathways, forests, meadows, streams and lakes as a dumping ground!

In many places the situation is so bad that the pristine beauty has been completely sullied. In this context the Rohtang pass, (13,500ft/4200m), above Manali in Himachal Pradesh, comes foremost to one's mind – a group of school children went on a clean-up drive and could collect 25kg waste, in less than a hour, and built a 'garbage-man' on the snow field to bring home the point to spectators!

The tourist is not entirely to blame for the litter that greets us almost everywhere – the locals certainly do contribute. However, the onus falls on us to set the standard and certainly not make things worse.

Over the years some of the basics that one has followed are outlined below. Unlike the rest of the book, which offers suggestions, I would like to urge you to strictly adhere to some rules, (and ensure that your co-travellers do the same), so you leave the environment you came to see as beautiful and well-preserved, as it should be.

Carry a waste bag in each vehicle. Eating and drinking is an essential part of any road journey, but all empty packets, bottles, cans etc. need to be kept in the vehicle. Get rid of the bag when you reach your destination, (provided disposal facilities are available there), or in a garbage dump en route.

While walking through the forest and munching a chocolate or a biscuit, ensure the wrapper is put in your pocket and got rid of later.

Apply the same rule while enjoying a drink and that great packed lunch by a rushing stream or a lovely meadow dotted with daisies. If you are a smoker be extremely careful with cigarette butts as this is the cause of many an unintended fire.

Avoid blasting music while driving or picnicking. Strongly discourage scribbling on trees, walls and buildings—we don't need to see cupid signs on every bench! Let the Himalayas make their impression on you and not the reverse!

For those who are going to be camping overnight: care has to be taken to ensure the use of kerosene or gas for cooking; toilet facilities should be at least 200ft away from a

Rhododendron in full bloom

water source; combustible waste such as paper and unlined cartons should be burned; biodegradable items such as food, should be buried, while non bio-degradables (plastic pouches, tetrapacks etc.) need to be carried back. While using a stream, or lake, for bathing minimise use of soap and washing of clothes with strong detergents.

When visiting temples or gompas, shorts, skirts and tight-fitting clothes should be avoided. Shoes need to be removed and avoid touching religious books or relics. Respect the sanctity of the religious places and their precious, fragile artifacts and refrain from photography when not permitted. It is advisable to ask permission before taking a photograph of the locals (in some areas, the camera is believed to capture the soul of the subject and photographs are a strict no-no).

Burn it, bury it or carry it out – be the invisible traveller! This is the best tribute you can pay the Himalayas ■

STAYING AND EATING RECOMMENDATIONS

HOTELS have been classified in various categories on the basis of tariff. We have, however, tried to provide some personal observations and you might at times find a C category hotel rated better than one in the A or B category.

A+	Rs. 5000 + for a double room
A	Rs. 3000 + for a double room
B	Rs. 1500 + for a double room
C	Below Rs. 1500

DARJEELING

Darjeeling has over 200 hotels in operation, ranging from the very classy to the very seedy. In season (April to June and October) demand can exceed supply and it is best to choose and book one's accommodation well in advance. We are providing some details on only ten of this multitude, though a list of around 100 others is part of Appendix A. The rates are full season rates and discounts up to 50% can be obtained off-season.

CATEGORY A+

▸▸ On top of our list, literally and figuratively, is the heritage *Windamere Hotel* perched atop the Observatory Hill. Far from the madding crowds that throng the Mall and Chowrasta, Windamere is simply the best-located hotel in Darjeeling with superb mountain and valley views even though the mighty Kanchendzonga is not visible. The spacious lay out and old world charm of this erstwhile boarding house for bachelor British tea planters is a recommendation in itself. Owned by the Tendufla family since the 1920s, Windamere was later converted to a hotel.

Some of the 37 double rooms now come with modern amenities such as cable TV and telephones as does one of the two 'honeymoon cottages'. There is a luxurious Raj-style lounge area with a well equipped bar and a comfortable dining room where the service and wonderful western cuisine bring the gracious clubs of yore to mind.

Those not staying can come for a meal (around Rs.600 per head) or a lavish English tea (around Rs.250 per head) on the sun drenched terraces. Prior notice is required for this and those carrying this book are likely to be given a 20% discount. Parking is available on the premises but recent traffic restrictions have stopped vehicular movement on the Mall which serves as the approach road, so be prepared for a short uphill trudge. If staying here, check the latest traffic restrictions so you are not sent around in circles by the somewhat rude and over efficient Darjeeling police!

P: 0354-2254041, 2254042 **F**: 2254043, 2254211
W: www.windamerehotel.com
E: reservations@windamerehotel.net

▸▸ *Mayfair Hill Resort*. Situated on a hillside just below the Raj Bhavan, this is another lush oasis in the concrete jungle that Darjeeling has grown into. The main building, which is a heritage structure, was originally owned by the illustrious William Lloyd and later acquired by the Maharaja of Nazargunj and converted into a resort in 1996. It boasts a comfortable and cozy library-cum- bar, a multi-cuisine restaurant and 7 rooms. Two blocks with 10 cottages each have been added making this a quiet, well laid out retreat midst lush plants and not many modern jarring notes.

The restaurant offers good Indian food (around Rs.500 per head) and residents have automatic access to the Darjeeling Gymkhana Club which offers roller skating, badminton, tennis, snooker and billiards. Parking is available in the premises but one has to reach the back entrance by a steeply descending road since the main entrance, opposite Raj Bhavan, is now reserved for VVIPs only!

P: 0354-2256376,2256476
F: 2252674 W: www.mayfairhotels.com
E: mayfairdarj@satyam.net.in

CATEGORY A

▸▸ *The New Elgin Hotel* is just below the Mall and though tastefully done up in a neo-colonial style, suffers from the fact that it is hemmed in by buildings. The rooms are comfortable and the ambience of its dining room, lounge and bar is distinctly old world. With 25 rooms and 2 suites, it also offers its own parking and is easily accessible as there are no traffic restrictions affecting its approach.

P: 0354-254114, 254267,254082 F: 0354-254267;
W: www.elginhotels.com E: newelgin@sify.com.

CATEGORY B

▸▸ *Sinclairs Hotel* is on Gandhi Road and is a typical modern building with 50 comfortable rooms, central heating and good service. The rooms on the top floor have excellent views of Mt. Kanchendzonga and in the front room you could actually watch the sunrise while lying in bed with a cuppa Darjeeling tea! Limited parking space is also available.

P: 0354-256431,256432,256948; F: 0354-254355;
E: darjeeling@sinclairshotels.com
W: www.sinclairshotels.com

CATEGORY C

▸▸ *The Darjeeling (Planters) Club* is one of Darjeeling's heritage landmarks. Located on Nehru Road just above the distinguished municipal building, this establishment dates back to 1868.

Started with the intention of providing a watering hole and accommodation for the sola topee and breeches clad British planters who rode into Darjeeling to escape the monotony of life on the tea estates. Accomodation is now open to all and it has 17 well furnished suites. Unlike the rest of Darjeeling, the Club does not suffer from a water shortage. With great snow views, an extremely central location, parking availability and easy access, the Club is excellent value for money.

P: 0354-2254348,2254349 F: 2254348;
E: thedarjeelingplantersclub@rediffmail.com

▸▸ *The Mahakal Palace*, behind Sinclairs Hotel, has 22 rooms, some in four bedroom cottages. The superior rooms have excellent mountain views.

P: 0354-2252026,2252056.

▸▸ *The Darjeeling Tourist Lodge* on Bhanu Sarani, close to St. Andrew's Church on the Mall, has 20 rooms and is in a quiet secluded location and has very good views. The only drawback is that it is owned and run by West Bengal Tourism Development Corporation and hence both cleanliness and service depend on the current manager in charge. Parking is available but accessibility depends on the traffic restrictions currently in force so you would need to check beforehand.

P: 0354-2254411,2254413 F: 0354-2254412.

▸▸ *Ivanhoe Hotel* is a heritage building with only 7 large comfortable rooms. Built as a manor house at the turn of the century it has colonial style fireplaces in each room and is centrally located, close to Mayfair, below the Mall. There is no parking within the premises and the approach is by the same sharply descending road you would use for Mayfair. P: 0354-2256082, 2255349.

▶▶ *The Main Old Bellevue Hotel* at Chowrasta has 43 rooms and some of these have good views.
P: 0354-2254075; **F**: 2254330
W: www.darjeelinghotels.com

▶▶ *Hotel Alice Villa* has 21 rooms and is located North of Chowrasta. For these two hotels in the Chowrasta, check on parking availability and traffic restrictions since this has been declared a 'no traffic' zone.
P: 0354-2254181, 2252098.

▶▶ The owners of *Taaja Restaurant*, that was earlier located in the Planters Club and has its main branch at Kolkata, are opening The Bonsai Hotel. It will provide 11 budget rooms with all basic amenities and is located just below the Planters Club. **P**: 0354-2256734

EATING OUT
EXPENSIVE
A meal or high tea at Windamere for the experience. Lunch or dinner at Mayfair.

AFFORDABLE
Lunch or dinner at Taaja's, the restaurant formerly at the Planters club, but now at 49 Laden La (Tel: 2256734)—the Kolkata branch was voted best restaurant of the year.

The bar at Buzz that has live music on several nights, followed by a meal at Glenarys. Originally started as a bakery in 1915 and known as Plivas, it was taken over and has been run by the Edwards family for over forty years now.

One can also visit Joey's Bar for a drink with great music videos, especially jazz, being played at just the right volume to allow one to have a conversation!

For old timers – Keventer's (just below Planters) has failed to keep up with the times—the food is average and the place is run down compared to the others.

GANGTOK
Hotels in Gangtok are mushrooming and have now crossed the century mark! Fortunately rates have not yet spiraled and there is good accommodation available at affordable prices. However, barring one, none of the hotels provide the hill station ambience with gardens to relax and enjoy the view—such spaces are found elsewhere in the city.

Rumtek, however, offers options with comfort, the right ambience and gardens to soak in the atmosphere. Where you choose to stay would depend on whether you want to be part of the action and enjoy the vibrancy of the bustling city despite the downside of crowds and traffic or if you prefer to take it easy and chill in Rumtek's sylvan surroundings and drive into Gangtok. The journey takes around forty-five minutes each way, so it is possible to visit Gangtok for the day and return to peace and tranquility for the night.

CATEGORY A
▶▶ *Nor-khill Hotel* on Palljor Stadium Road is a little away from the crowded area. Built in 1932 by the Chogyal, it was used to receive and entertain Heads of State and other dignitaries. Now a resort with 25 rooms it has pleasant valley views and this is the only property that has gardens where one can relax with some element of privacy. Travel agents try to push the package that includes all meals (around Rs.5000 per night for a couple), but since there are some good eating places in town we would recommend going for a non-meal option at around Rs.4000 per night.
P: 03592-205637; **F**: 03592-25639

W: www.elginhotels.com **E**: norkhill@sify.com

▸▸ *The Royal Plaza* is part of the Sarovar group and this is Gangtok's largest (55 rooms) and most modern hotel. With central heating and good valley views, you can forgive the concrete structure. They also have a good multi-cuisine restaurant.

P: 03592-280032/232
E: trp@sarovarparkplaza.com
W: www.theroyalplazahotel.com

CATEGORY B

▸▸ *Tashi Delek*. Located on M.G. Road, in the heart of town, the alley-like entrance with an ornate doorway opens into an opulent lobby, decorated elaborately in the Tibetan style. Some of the 50 double rooms have great snow views, particularly those on the upper deck. The other rooms are located downstairs from the lobby and the first time around that feels kind of strange! The overall décor in the suites and some of the rooms is over-the-top, but the peaceful open-air terrace, good food, and the location are adequate compensation. Approach to the hotel is closed between 5 and 8 p.m. and parking is available outside the hotel. However, vehicles of a slightly larger size, like a Scorpio or Qualis, cannot be parked here even in the day as they are

Mt. Narsing Village Resort in Ravangla

considered a hindrance to the approach of fire-engine trucks in case of an emergency. Inconvenient as the rule closing traffic between 5-8 p.m. may appear, one certainly enjoys the feeling of a pedestrian-only market place. However, there is no denying the urgent need for convenient parking as well as for tourists to be forewarned so they do not arrive tired and weary to face the rude shock of having to offload and go in search for parking space.
P: 03592-202038,2024156/57/58; **F**: 03592-202362; **W**: www.hoteltashidelek.com
E: htd@hoteltashidelek.com

▸▸ *Chumbi Residency* is a modern hotel with 25 rooms, built only nine years ago. The rooms are comfortable, some with good views and a pleasant restaurant on the top floor. Located on Tibet Road, above M.G. Road, parking is available and the peaceful Ridge area is only a short climb away.
P: 03592-226618/19/20; **F**: 03592-222707; **E**: slg_chumbi@sancharnet.in.

▸▸ *Netuk House* is opposite Chumbi Residency on Tibet Road. Do not let the external façade of this building deter you - once you step in it is a veritable oasis midst the bleak concrete urbanisation around. Home to the Denzongpa family, this heritage property has been converted to a small, exclusive hotel with 11 rooms and is the closest you will come to experience traditional Sikkimese family hospitality and cuisine. The best rooms are the two on top of the dining area, and the three on the upper floor of the annexe though the ones in the back of the main building are large, comfortable and sun-drenched. The garden terrace has great views of the city and the snow capped mountains. Parking is available on the premises.

P: 03592-202374; **F**: 226778
E: slg_netuk@sancharnet.in

▸▸ *Hotel Tibet* on P.S. Road has 32 rooms, of which 17 have good views. Its multi-cuisine restaurant is probably the best in Gangtok, and the hotel itself is centrally located.
P: 03592-202523,203468;
F: 03592-226233 **W**: www.sikkiminfo.net /hoteltibet **E**: htltibet@yahoo.com

▸▸ *New Castle Hotel* in the Deorali area is on the main N.H.31 and is only two years old. The rooms are comfortable, some have decent valley views, but parking is a hassle. The restaurant, Porky's, has excellent chicken sizzlers.
P: 03592-281707,281715; **F**: 03592-281908
E: ncinfous@yahoo.com

CATEGORY C

▸▸ *Sonam Delek* on Tibet Road, (close to Netuk House), has 15 rooms of which 6 have great views and are excellent value for money.
P: 03592-202566, 228906
F: 03592-203197; **W**: www. sikkiminfo.com/ sonamdelek **E**: slg_hsdelek@sancharnet.in

▸▸ *Hotel Aleya* at Zero Point is not hemmed in by buildings and some of the rooms have good views.
P: 03592-205316.

▸▸ *Denzong Inn*, located in the heart of the city, close to the three main bazaars, has 22 cosy rooms.
P: 03592-202692; **F**: 03592-202362
E: tashidelek@sikkim.org

▸▸ *Norbu Ghang* with its 21 rooms is located opposite Hotel Tibet, and the upper rooms have decent views
P: 03592-202237,223537.

▸▸ *Hotel Sai Kripa* is a welcome addition, offering excellent value for money. This centrally located hotel has all modern amenities including a well stocked bar and a restaurant.

P: 03592-201477, 201470
E: hotelsaikripa@yahoo.co.in

RUMTEK
CATEGORY B

▸▸ *Shambala Mountain Resort* is ideally located just a stones throw away from the main Rumtek Monastery. With 3 cottages and 12 tastefully appointed rooms this is a place where you can put up your feet and relax. The dining area opens out onto a patio, with lawns descending in terraces to a brook that flows through the property. Extremely convenient for day journeys to the nearby monasteries, the Ipecac Garden and for seeing the sights of Gangtok and then escaping to beautiful, natural environs.
P: 03592-252440,252243 F: 03592-252241
E: sikkim@ahmedindia.com

▸▸ *Martam Village Resort* is 6 km beyond the main monastery and has 10 well appointed, thatched cottages set on the hillside. Completely isolated this is a good place to relax and spend some time in. The hillside is lush green and the huts set in a way that privacy is maintained. P: 03592-203314,236843
F: 03592-204391 E: slg_martam@sancharnet.in

CATEGORY C

▸▸ *Teen Talay* is a recently built resort with 7 rooms of which 3 are in the main building and the rest in two double-unit cottages. Located 1km before the Rumtek Monastery, you turn off at the Ani Gompa and a 0.5 km drivable trail brings you to this cozy resort set amongst 6 acres of rolling hills with great views of Gangtok by night.
P: 03592-252256, 098-320-14867
E: sikkimresort@hotmail.com

CATEGORY D

▸▸ *Sungay Guest House* with only 6 rooms is located just inside the monastery gates. Rooms with a view, are spartan, but are a steal at Rs. 200 per night for someone not looking for trappings. P: 03592-252221

EATING OUT

Gangtok offers a choice of multi-cuisine restaurants that maintain a good standard in food while being reasonably priced.

▸▸ *The Snow Lion* at *Hotel Tibet* rates highly for its food, particularly the momos that are most succulent. *Tashi Delek* has good Indian fare, as also an elaborate traditional Sikkimese meal (but 24 hrs. advance notice is required for this). The *Chumbi Residency* has good Indian, tandoori, cuisine. The *Blue Sheep*, at the beginning of M.G. Road, has good soups and continental food. *House of Bamboo*, just beyond the Eastern end of M.G. Road, in the *Hotel Neptune* premises, has great atmosphere, good music and is a favourite of the local youngsters. *Baker's Café* on M.G. Road has a good confectionery, pizzas and a lively, peppy atmosphere. *Porky's* at Deorali has the best chicken sizzlers and have just started an exclusively Sikkimese cuisine section. *Little Italy* is a cute bar in the same area while Fusion *Bar* with its adjoining disco, 'Time Out', are in the Tadong area (4km from the center). Since public transport is operational till 10 p.m. it is best to make secure arrangements in advance if you plan to be out later.

RUMTEK: If only visiting the monasteries, stop for lunch at *Shambala Resort* and relax in the gardens afterwards. The dhabas outside the monastery serve very ordinary fare and are best avoided.

Staying and Eating Recommendations

DRINK

Try the local millet/barley 'wine', known as Chang and served in a wooden cask with a bamboo straw – the milky brew is locally also known as Tombu. The concoction gets weaker as you add more water but don't underestimate its benign slightly sour flavor!

KALIMPONG

CATEGORY A

▸ *Hotel Silver Oaks* belongs to the Elgin group and affords views of Kanchendzonga on a clear day. Sitting in the quaint gazebos set amidst the flowering garden is indeed a magical experience! The rooms are well appointed and comfortable. Built in 1930, it was at one time the residence of the prominent architect Frederick Desraj who built the old Teesta bridge.
P: 03552-255296/255766/7
W: www.elginhotels.com

CATEGORY B

▸ *Himalayan Hotel* is a beautiful, stately, heritage building in stone with oak ceilings, teak pillars and period furniture. This was the home of David McDonald who went to Lhasa as an interpreter on the Younghusband Mission in 1905, was later posted as the British Trade Agent and finally retired here with his family. He later converted their home into a hotel and it has, to date, been managed by the family. There are eight double rooms in the main building but even the adjacent two new blocks that house an additional eight rooms have been very tastefully built. There are open fireplaces in most rooms and the garden is very well laid out with a variety of seasonal flowers midst lush green plants and has excellent views of the mountain peaks.

P: 03552-255248, 258602 **F**: 03552-255122
E: info@yahimalanhotel.biz

CATEGORY C

▸ *Morgan House* probably has the best location in town, perched as it is atop Darpin Hill with astounding views of both the mountain peaks and valleys. The building is a graciously proportioned heritage structure in ivy-covered stone. The West Bengal Tourism Dev. Corp. manages the hotel and though amenities are basic, with a bit of a run down look about it, the tariff is reasonable. They have five standard double rooms and two small/single rooms.
P: 03552-255384 **W**: www.wbtourism.com/ www.westbengaltourism.com
E: wbtdc@cal2.vsnl.net.in

LACHEN/LACHUNG

In Lachen the accommodation is basic but comfortable in the family run Gurudongmar Lodge. The army has a guesthouse for their visitors and the best place to stay if you can manage an invitation!
▸ In Lachung, *Marcopolo Travels* have constructed the 5-storied, concrete, *Snow Lion Mountain Resort* that unfortunately sticks out like a sore thumb in this pristine location. The rooms on the top floor have good views. The food is simple but wholesome fare.
P: Marcopolo Travels – 03592-204116, 229407
F: 03592-205078; **W**: www.worldmarcopolo.com
E: kats@sancharnet.in/ infor@worldmarcopolo.com

MIRIK

▸ *Mirik Orange County Resort*, run by the owners of Glenarys in Darjeeling, has 12 stone cottages on a hilltop with very good Himalayan views.

P: 0354-2257554, 2257556 **W**: www.glenarys.net;
E: glens_getaways@sancharnet.in

PELLING

In ten years Pelling has transformed itself from a sleepy little hamlet to a bustling resort with over 50 hotels vying for prime space, offering mountain views and ending up just crowding each other out!

CATEGORY B

▸▸ *Norbhu Ghang Resort*: Set in a stand-alone location, just above the football ground, this is the only classy place in Pelling. The approach is a bit confusing, as one has to drive across the football field (interrupting a match that may be in progress!), but once inside the compound you are completely cut off from the outside world. It has 21 rooms, built as cottages tucked into the hill face at various levels. With well laid out pathways and gardens, this is a great place to relax and enjoy the spectacular panorama of the Kanchendzonga range at sunrise. From some rooms (503,504,802 & 803) one has to literally draw the curtain to witness this unforgettable spectacle. The main block has 9 rooms but we recommend the cottages as they provide privacy and also because some have their own private garden set between two cottages. Service is good, but the standard of cuisine doesn't quite match the place and could do with some improvement. The 'chang' served in the bar is definitely worth trying but remember to give them advance notice for this.

P: 03595-258272,250566 **F**: 03595-258271
E: norbughang@sancharnet.in

▸▸ *Elgin Mt. Pandim* is the newest kid on the block, having taken over the premises from the government which ran it till 2006. The property is adjacent to the Pemayangtse Monastery and was till the recent past the only place to stay in Pelling. Vis-à-vis location this is still the best property in Pelling with the most stunning views, particularly at sunrise as you are closer to the peaks than anywhere else in Pelling. Having been refurbished, the hotel has gained immensely in ambience, comfort and cuisine.

P: 03595-270576.

CATEGORY C

▸▸ *Hotel Norbu Ghang* is a poorer cousin of the above mentioned resort and is at the tri-junction of the roads leading to Dentam, Yuksom and Geysing. The rooms are clean and comfortable and some have good views.

P: 03595-258216, 258555 **F**: 03595-258271

▸▸ *Hotel Phamrong*, is named after the cascading waterfall, visible on the distant hillside, where the female Boddhisattava 'Dorje Phamo' meditated and bathed. It is adjacent to Hotel Norbu Ghang and has 25 clean and comfortable rooms. Those with a view offer excellent value for money and a multi-cuisine restaurant is being set up. The young owner, Utpal Yongda, is an enthusiastic guide with good local knowledge – his sister owns Netuk House in Gangtok.

P: 03595-250660,25821; **F**: 03595-258281
E: mailphamrong@yahoo.com

▸▸ There is a PWD bungalow on the same hill as Mt. Pandim that commands an equally fantastic view. Bookings have to be made from Gangtok but the effort may well be worth making.

EATING

There are a number of small eateries in Pelling and as is typical of a popular, small tourist locale, you can get anything from South Indian to Bengali cuisine! Some of the cafés have nice terraces to sit out on and though, in general, the food is not much to write home about, it is certainly very palatable.

YUKSOM / GEYZING

If you plan to spend some time in the same general area, the *Hotel Tashigang*, in Yuksom provides a great ambience and good comfortable rooms and this is the base for many of the well-known treks in Sikkim.

The owner of Tashigang has recently opened a resort, outside Geyzing and below the Rabdentse Palace ruins.

P: 03595-241202,241203 (Yuksom); 03595-250340 (Geyzing); or 09811014490

RAVANGLA
CATEGORY C

▶ *Mt. Narsing Village Resort* is located 3km from the main town, on the road to Kewzing/Legship. At a lofty 6400ft this resort offers a mix of budget and good accommodation. We recommend staying in the twin room cottages located 1.5km up the hillside. The views are spectacular, the food good and it is a great place to relax in. This is also a good base to visit the Tashiding and Ralong monasteries and for the treks to Maenem and Tendong hill. Warning! The road up is a steep twisting dirt track but the nail biting drive is worth it.

P: 03595-260558 **E**: takapa@sancharnet.in

SHOPPING IN GANGTOK

The Cottage Industries Emporium at Zero Point has a variety of hand woven carpets, shawls, blankets in traditional weaves, as well as other items such as handmade paper and exquisitely carved wooden tables.

Another place well worth a visit is *Babu Kazi Sakya's* shop next to the entrance to Tashi Delek Hotel on M.G. Road. This is a treasure trove for those wanting to drool at antiques and artifacts from this region and though the prices may seem high, some good bargaining will get you much better prices that you would able to get for similar stuff in Ladakh.

MEDICAL FACILITIES

Gangtok has a government hospital and a good private one run by the Manipal group. There are district hospitals at Namchi, Gyalsing and Mangan but in other places medical facilities are practically non-existent. Pelling has private doctors but in North Sikkim, the army is the main back up. Darjeeling has several private practitioners and a civil hospital, as does Siliguri, but the closest for serious ailments is Kolkata ■

FOOD

Gangtok and Pelling both have a wide choice of cuisine available, so you need only consider carrying goodies to supplement your basic meals at Lachen/Lachung, as also for picnic lunches en route.

A fairly good variety of canned items are available in Gangtok including the Gouda cheese made

Do not overload yourself, you may find the walk up to the monasteries rough going

locally in W. Sikkim.

However, the more exotic food items you might want to indulge yourself with should be carried from your home as even Siliguri does not extend to this.

What to carry

DRINKS

Liquor is freely available in Gangtok and Pelling. There is a good local brand of dark, as well as white rum, and the old faithful – 'Old Monk' – is very available.

The local beer, Dansberg, made by a brewery promoted by the popular film star Danny Denzongpa, is also extremely palatable. Other hard liquor is easy to come by but it is best to stock up for your travels out of Gangtok.

The local 'chang', or millet wine, is served in many places and definitely worth sampling. Bottled water and cold drinks are available en route except in Lachen/Lachung, so Chungthang is the place to stock up.

CLOTHING

Warm clothes to cope with very cold conditions albeit for short periods are a must, as also warm socks and sensible walking shoes. Ideally one should dress in layers so that one can add and shed as per the conditions – for a fair amount of the day a cotton shirt will be enough. The sight of some tourists in dhotis and chappals at Nathu La was enough to induce a shiver inside our parkas. If you are visiting in the period April to September, remember to carry some rain gear or do the local economy some good by buying umbrellas from Lal Bazaar in Gangtok.

MEDICINES

There are plenty of chemists in Gangtok but you should carry a small stock of essentials including Paracetemol, Combiflam, your choice of medicine for stomach upsets, motion sickness, antiseptic cream and bandaids for minor cuts. Also add a good sun block lotion.

If advised by your doctor, oxygen can be carried – portable lightweight cylinders are now available.

While walking through the forest, carrying a pouch of salt is a useful precaution to take – at certain times of the year, particularly the rainy season, leeches are common. If you are unlucky to be one of their 'victims' the best way to get rid of these irritating specimens is to sprinkle salt at the point where it has attached itself – it will fall off within a short time. Pulling at it is a no-no as part of it will remain under your skin and cause discomfort.

GENERAL

Binoculars and cameras are essential – film is available in Gangtok and Pelling.

One may also carry a mosquito repellant – the liquid or mat type will do.

A small torch and a Swiss Army knife may also come handy ■

PERMITS FOR SIKKIM

BEING a border state three types of permits are required for foreign visitors, whereas Indian nationals require permits only for areas beyond Chungthang in North Sikkim and for visiting Tsomgo, Menmecho and Nathu La in East Sikkim.

INNER LINE PERMITS

These are no longer required by Indians, but are a must for foreigners before they can enter Sikkim. However, this is not a problem as these are issued without any fuss by all Indian missions abroad as also in New Delhi, Chennai, Kolkata and Mumbai at the Foreigners Regional Registration Office. In addition these are also available at the Sikkim government offices in New Delhi, Kolkata and Siliguri. These permits are valid for fifteen days and can be extended for another fifteen days thrice in Sikkim from the Superintendant of Police in the North, South and West districts as also the FRO in Gangtok. These permits are issued on the spot on production of photocopies of the passport with a valid visa and two passport photographs.

RESTRICTED AREA PERMITS

These are required by Indians as well as foreigners for visiting most areas of tourist interest in North Sikkim, as also areas close to Gangtok such as Tsomgo and Menmecho lakes as also the Nathu La pass. These are also required if one is planning on doing the trek upto Zongri in West Sikkim. These permits are easily organised by your local tour operator but foreigners are required to travel in a group of at least two people.

PROHIBITED AREA PERMITS

These are required for treks to areas such as Green Lake or for climbing Mt. Kanchendzonga! Permission is available only from the Ministry of Home Affairs in Delhi and are not easily available ■

ACUTE MOUNTAIN SICKNESS (AMS)

ACUTE mountain sickness is a condition brought about by decreased oxygen content in the blood due to lower atmospheric pressure at high altitudes.

Oxygen normally flows from the alveoli, (air sacs) of the lungs, into the blood as the pressure in the alveoli is greater than that in the blood. At higher altitudes, the lower pressure of oxygen in the atmosphere reduces pressure of oxygen in the blood – at 18,000ft/5500m, the blood oxygen pressure is 40–45mm, which is half the normal value.

The development of symptoms of AMS depend upon the rate of ascent, elevation attained, and most importantly—individual susceptibility. AMS can be of the mild (benign) or severe (malignant) type. Symptoms usually start twelve to twenty-four hours after arrival and begin to decrease in severity on about the third day.

The symptoms of mild AMS include headaches, dizziness, loss of appetite, lethargy, and difficulty in sleeping. The treatment calls for rest as much as for staying at the same altitude till the symptoms disappear – which they normally should by the third day. Paracetamol together with a Combiflam drowned with a litre of water can be taken for the headaches, while Stemitil (5mg) helps nausea.

Malignant AMS can develop from mild AMS and can be fatal. The symptoms include breathlessness, double vision, severe headaches which do not respond to Paracetemol, confusion and irrational behavior, and a dry cough that may progress to production of a pink frothy substance. The treatment for this is immediate descent to a

View from Pelling

lower altitude – even 500m can produce substantial relief. In addition medication is also recommended – Decadron 8mg to start with, followed by 4mg doses six hourly as also Depin 20 mg six hourly.

Whereas starting a course of a medicine called Diamox before going on your trip is a precaution recommended by some, others believe the medicine masks the symptoms if AMS does occur and can lead to delayed treatment. If you are an anxious traveller wanting to take additional precautions, we suggest you consult a doctor on this medication since there is some controversy over its use.

In order to avoid AMS besides

ascending slowly and resting at progressively higher altitudes the following guidelines are very important:

» Fluid intake of 4-5 litres spread out during the day is essential this can be started 48 hours before one's ascent to altitudes above 10,000ft.

» The diet should be carbohydrate rich and not high on proteins. Heavy meals should be avoided.

» As a general rule, one's night halt should be at an altitude lower than the peak achieved during the day.

» Avoid alcohol as it dehydrates one; remember what happens when one has imbibed on a flight – the cabin is pressurised at the equivalent of 5000ft but one still gets dehydrated pretty quickly!

» Similarly, you should abstain from smoking as it impairs one's breathing in the rarefied air.

» Your regular exercise routine is to be avoided till acclimatisation is complete and you feel absolutely normal.

Despite all precautions, it is still possible to have symptoms of AMS – the important thing is to recognise them and treat them accordingly. Generally AMS occurs at altitudes above 11,000ft/3500m but cases at 10,000ft have been known.

The writer undertook the journey to Leh by road with a large group of thirteen adults and six children (aged five to fifteen). We followed all the rules outlined above but one afternoon, which stretched into a long night, mild symptoms of AMS hit almost eighty percent of the group when we spent the night at 14,000ft. Treatment with Paracetamol, fluid intake and early to bed restored everyone to near normal by the next morning. The other strange thing about AMS is that it can hit even the most experienced mountaineer, who has had no previous history, at random – so please do not assume that if you have been there and done it that you are immune!!

AMS AND HOMEOPATHY

Homeopaths recommend the use of coca for headaches caused by altitude.

Ferrum Phos 30C is a great remedy to 'give oxygen' – dose as needed. If seriously short of oxygen, use every five minutes to 'catch up'. five to ten doses like that is usually effective.

Be sure to eat a diet supporting quick blood building – Lixotinic is good supplement that not only has the iron to make haemoglobin but copper to help it absorb. Good aerobic fitness is also necessary to increase red blood cells ■

DRIVING TIPS

SOME PRECAUTIONS THAT MAY PROVE VERY USEFUL

▸▸ If you are driving your own car, switching to tubeless tyres is strongly recommended. Both road conditions and new cars today make it possible to reach a speed of 100 kmph, and more, on some stretches. A front tyre blowing out, in such situations, could mean very serious trouble. Tubeless tyres have the twin advantage of deflating slowly and being capable of inflation that would allow you to drive up to 60km or more till you reach a repair shop.

▸▸ One should also carry a do-it-yourself repair kit. This is a very handy, if not necessary accessory to carry as small towns are not yet familiar with tubeless technology. A small air pump that plugs into the cigarette lighter socket is also available and, depending on the type, costs between Rs. 2000 and 6000.

▸▸ Carrying an additional spare tyre may seem a little extreme, but if you are not using tubeless tyres, can be very useful when travelling in remote terrain where one may not come across an air pump or repair shop for several hours at a stretch.

▸▸ Also carry a couple of spare tubes as the specific one for your vehicle may not be available everywhere.

▸▸ If you have a luggage carrier, add a 20 litre jerry can of additional fuel as a contingency measure – sometimes all does not go according to plan and the scheduled refuelling stop could be dry.

▸▸ Carry spare engine belts, if your car still uses them, as also clutch and accelerator cables.

▸▸ A charger that plugs into the cigarette lighter socket is extremely useful for charging cameras and cell phones while on the move.

Above all, remember that in the tourist season there are a large number of inexperienced drivers from the plains hitting the hill roads and not conversant, or comfortable with 'hill-driving-norms' – so be cautious, and take those curves carefully ▪

TRAVEL AND TOUR OPERATORS

GANGTOK has over fifty travel operators who are recognised by the government of Sikkim, but most operate from hole-in-the-wall offices and it is advisable to have your own travel agent interface with an appropriate local operator.

We are giving details of two Gangtok based travel operators who we found reliable and efficient.

▸ *Yuksom Tours and Travels* Borong House, Above Telephone Exchange, Gangtok. P: 03592-226822; F: 03592-220960 E: takapa@sancharnet.in W: www.yuksom-tours.com. The owner of Mt. Narsing Resort at Ravangla is also a tour operator, specialising in the W. Sikkim area. He organises holidays – stay, travel, sightseeing et al, including moderate treks if that's what you are looking for.

▸ *Marcopolo World Travels* P.S. Road, Gangtok-737101. P: 03592 - 204116, 229407; F: 03592/205078; E: kats@sancharnet.in W: www.worldmarcopolo.com They specialise in travel to North Sikkim and also have their own establishments to stay at in Lachen and Lachung.

SILIGURI

▸ *Heat Travel and Tours*, Shiv Mahal, 34 Bidyasagar Road, Khalpara, Siliguri-734405. P: 0353-2504631-643; F: 0353-2503630 E: heat@sancharnet.in It is difficult not to be satisfied with the indefatigable Deepak Gupta and his team. Based at Siliguri, with branch offices in Darjeeling and Gangtok, they are extremely capable of making your holiday work without any major glitches. They also have a good tie up for rafting on the Teesta with Action Adventure and Rescue Group, run by the very competent Sukbir Tamang.

DELHI

▸ *Ibex Expeditions*, run by Mandip (Mandy) Soin and his wife Anita – this personalised, knowledgeable service is difficult to beat. Mandip is a climber and the benefit of his personal experience in planning a trek or even a simple holiday is of great help. Having been in the business for twenty-five years, they have seen it, done it and can handle things to perfection (Steam pudding served for dessert on a walk at 15,000ft!!) G-66 East of Kailash, New Delhi - 110065, India. P: 91-11-26912641, F: 26846403 E: ibex@nde.vsnl.net.in W: www.ibexexpeditions.com

▸ *The Big Boys* a.k.a. *Travel Corporation of India, Sita World Travels, Cox and King* and others. The advantage is that they probably operate in the city you live in, and are therefore more accessible. However, in this age of communication by e-mail and low STD tariffs, this advantage isn't necessarily a key issue. Does size matter? Maybe. Particularly if you make up your mind at the last minute to take off somewhere and bookings in the hotel you want to stay in and/or air tickets aren't available. They may have the clout to make things happen, when others have given you the thumbs down

BANGALORE

▸▸ *Hammock Leisure Holiday Pvt. Ltd.* was set up to 10 years ago by a group of young professionals from the service industry. With branches in Cochin and Mumbai and associate office in Chennai they are well placed to customise your holiday. 314/1 Vijay Kiran, 7th Cross Domlur Layout, Bangalore.
P: 25351877/25351444;
E: hammock@vsnl.net
W: www.hammockholidays.com ▪

SIKKIM TOURISM OFFICES
GANGTOK
Sikkim Tourist Information Centre
M G Marg, Gangtok-737101
P: 03592-221634
F: 03592-205647

Sikkim Tourism Development Corporation (STDC)
M.G Marg, Gangtok-737101
P: 03592-222634, 220352
F: 222362

SIKKIM GOVERNMENT TOURIST OFFICES
NEW DELHI
New Sikkim House
14, Panchsheel Marg, Chanakyapuri
New Delhi-110021
P: 011-26115346, 26115171

SILIGURI
SNT Colony, Hill Cart Road
Siliguri
P: 0353-2512646

NEW JALPAIGURI
NJP Railway Station
New Jalpaiguri
P: 0353-2690475

BAGDOGRA
Bagdogra Airport Terminal Bldg.
Bagdogra
P: 0353-2551036

KOLKATA
4/1, Middleton Street
Kolkata-700016
P: 033-22815328

Website: www.sikkimtourism.org

APPENDIX

Since it is impossible to list all hotels, restaurants and travel agencies, visitors are advised to check with the Tourist Information Center, TASS of SH&RA Gangtok, for detailed and complete information. This guide is for information only and does not suggest preferences. The publishers are not liable for any inconvenience caused by information contained herein.

Tariffs are on European Plan (double occupancy/standard rooms) and exclude taxes and service charges. Please re-confirm the latest tariff and available discounts with the management of the hotels prior to reservation or check-in.

RS. 2000+++

NAME OF HOTEL	LOCATION	PHONE(S)
Netuk House	Tibet Road	222374 / 226778
Norkhill Hotel	P.S. Road	225637 / 225639
Tashi Delek	New Market	222038 / 222991

RS.1000+++

Central Hotel	Opp. Super Market	222105 / 222553
Cherry Guest House	Church Road	225431 / 229652
Chumbi Residency	Tibet Road	226618 / 226619
Hotel Asian Heights	Kazi Road	227547 / 227548
Hotel Bayul	M.G. Road	224649
Hotel Golden Heights	M. Marg	221858
Hotel Golden Nest	Nam-Nang	227008 / 227035
Hotel Heruka	31 N.H. Way	280073 / 280793
Hotel Rendezvous	31 N.H. Way	226271/72-73-74
Hotel Swagat	P.S. Road	224295 / 227751
Hotel Tibet	P.S. Road	222523 / 224962
The New Castle	Deorali	281707 / 281908
The Oriental	New Market	221180 / 81/82

RS. 500 TO RS. 900

Agarwal's Central Point Lodge	NH 31A	222117
Denzong Inn	Lall Market	222692
Glacier Guest House	M.G. Marg	222137 / 228561
Hotel Anola	M.G. Marg	224233 / 223238
Hotel Dew Pond	P.S. Road	223905 / 227292
Hotel Gochala	Kazi Road	223634
Hotel Golden Nest	Nam-Nang	227008 / 227035
Hotel Golden Pagoda	M.G. Road	226928 / 226929
Hotel Magnolia	NH 31A	224687 / 227749
Hotel Marigold	NH 31A	23951 / 224089
Hotel Migtin	M.G. Road	224101
Hotel Mount Jopuno	P.S. Road	223502 / 228239
Hotel Mount Simov	Tadong	270956
Hotel Mylong	Pani House	280446
Hotel Norbu Ghang	P.S. Road	222237 / 223537
Hotel Pineridge	Namnang	224958
Hotel Pomra	Secretariat Road	226648
Hotel Sonam Delek	S.G. Road	222566 / 228906
Hotel Soyang	New Market	222331
Hotel Staywell	NH 31A	23563
Hotel Teesta Rangit	New Market	225609 / 228335

►► Hotel Tip Top (Gurathi Food)	D.P.H. Road	226229
►► Hotel View Point	NH 31A	222549 / 228579
►► Hotel Zam-Den	Old Children's Park	24997
►► Hotel Zi	Tibet Road	225481
►► Hungry Jack	NH 31A	28138
►► Mintokling Guest House	Bhanu Path	224226
►► Mist Tree Mountain	P.S. Road	223827 / 224263
►► Park Residency	Near Super Mkt.	228410 / 228411
►► Sukhim Guest House	Namnang	223796 / 227272
►► Sunny Guest House	NH 31A	222179
►► The Dzong	M.G. Road	220279 / 220281
►► The Seasons Hotel	Namnang Road	280288

BELOW RS. 500

►► Darshan Lodge	Pani House	280876
►► Gangtok Lodge	M.G. Marg	226562
►► Green Hotel	M.G. Marg	224439 / 225057
►► Hotel Alaya	Zero Point	225316
►► Hotel Annapurna	New Market	224877
►► Hotel Bayul	M.G. Marg	224649
►► Hotel Ben	New Market	224877
►► Hotel Holiday Hill	P.S. Road	222750
►► Hotel Kanishka	Opp. Bus Stand	224011 / 224690
►► Hotel Lhakar	P.S. Road	225708 / 227082
►► Hotel Natraj	Deorali	280799 / 280550
►► Hotel Pardick		220835
►► Hotel Ritz International	NH 31A	225128
►► Hotel Siddharth	New Market	221009 / 224807
►► Hotel Sonar Tari	Deorali	280986
►► Hotel Yumthang	Church Road	223841
►► Kabur Inn Lodge	Tibet Road	224149
►► Kanchen View	Pani Road	281762 / 280763
►► Millennium Inn	DPH Road	228617
►► Nahan Lodge	Church Road	228241
►► New Green Hotel	Balwakhani	224060
►► New Orchid Guest House	Dev. Area	221063
►► Pomra Lodge	Bhanu Path	223479 / 226648
►► Potala Hotel	Tibet Road	222440
►► Primula Lodge	Church Road	225496
►► Samphet Hotel	Dev. Area	228677
►► Quality Lodge	Deorali	280515
►► Twilight Lodge	31 N.H. Way	224352 / 223225

HOME STAY

►► Borong House	Above Tel. Exchange	226822
►► Kewzing Home	Lower Dev. Area	223702 / 225735

RESORTS

Resorts in and around Gangtok are approximately between forty-five minutes to an hour's drive from the city. The resorts mentioned here have aesthetically designed traditional cottages. With the increase in tourist traffic, more resorts are being established around the countryside. For a true pastoral taste of Sikkim coupled with tranquility these resorts are worth a try.

›› Martam Village Resort	Upper Martam	223314 / 236843
›› Sapten Adventure Center	Lingdum Basty	227979
›› Sanghiling Resorts	Tashi View Point	237540 / 237201
›› Shambhala Mt. Resort	Rumtek	252240 / 252243
›› The Bamboo Resort	Sajong, Rumtek	252516 / 95353 202049

HOTELS IN DARJEELING

Since it is impossible to list all hotels, restaurants and travel agencies, visitors are advised to check with the Tourist Information Center at Darjeeling for detailed and complete information. This guide is for information only and does not suggest preferences. The publishers are not liable for any inconvenience caused by information contained herein.

Please re-confirm the latest tariff and available discounts with the management of the hotels prior to reservation or check-in.

NAME	ADDRESS	PHONE / FAX
›› Hotel Abhisatya	147, Dr Zakir Hussain Road	2254459
›› Hotel Akanksha	18/1, T.N. Road	2253532
›› Hotel Alice Villa	H.D. Lama Road	2254181 / 2252098
›› Hotel Aliment	40, Dr Zakir Hussain Road	2255068
›› Andy's Guest House	102, Dr Zakir Hussain Road	22531256
›› Hotel Anandan	1/1, T.N. Road	2255063
›› Anjuman E Islamia	Guest House Botanical Road	2252971
›› Hotel New Annapurna	6, Gandhi Road	--
›› Hotel Apsara	6, Ladenia Road	2252242 / 2252983 F: 2254484
›› Hotel The Attic	50, Uday Chand Road	2252120
›› Hotel Bellevue	1, Nehru Road	2254075
›› Hotel Broadway	4, Cooch Behar Road	2253248 / 2256270
›› Buddhist Lodge	47/1, Ladenla Road	2254710
›› Hotel Camino	106, Gandhi Road	2252869
›› Hotel Capital	1-A, Rockville Road	2254160 / 2254698
›› Cedar Inn	Jalapahar Road	2254446 / 2253598
›› Hotel Chalet	Chowrasta, The Mall	2254072
›› Classic Guest House	C.R. Das Road	2254106 / 2254904
›› Continental Hotel	58, Gandhi Road	2253196 / 2253618
›› Cosy Home	17, Nehru Road	2254074
›› Crystal Palace Hotel	H.D. Lama Road	2253317
›› Darjeeling Gymkharna	The Mall	2254392
›› Darjeeling Guest House	16, D.B. Giri Road	2256327
›› Darjeeling Hotel	4-A, Belombre Road	2252314
›› DCM Lodge	18, B.M. Chatterjee Road	2252375
›› Dekeling Hotel	51, Gandhi Road	2254159 / 2253298 F: 2253298
›› Dekeling Resort	2, A.J.C. Bose Road	2254159, 2253347, 2253092 (F:2253298)
›› Dil Hotel	12-A, Rockville Road	2252773
›› Dragon Lodge	14, H.D. Lama Road	2256234
›› Hotel Fairmount	10, Gandhi Road	2253646 F: 2253647
›› Fortune Hotel	Mountain Holidays	2256048-49
›› Fortune Resort Central		2258721-22-23

NAME	ADDRESS	PHONE / FAX
Hotel Garuda	64, Ladenla Road	2254562-63 (F: 2256110)
Himgiri Lodge	16, H.D. Lama Road	2254852
Hotel Imperial	Judge Bazar	2253605 / 2254819/
		2253495
Hotel Ivonhoe	Franklyan Prestage Road	2256082 / 2255349
Janta Lodge	16, H.D. Lama Road	2254507
Hotel Kadambari	Goody Road (below Rly. Stn.)	2253564
Kailash Hotel (opp. Rly Stn.)	15-A, Hill Cart Road	2256425
Hotel Lunar	51, Gandhi Road	2254194-95
		F: 2257013
Hotel Mahakal	Robertson Road	2253564
Hotel Mahamaya	104/1, Rockville Road	2254700
Hotel Mayfair	16-Rock ville Road	2256272
Mishra's (North Star) Hotel	11, H.D. Lama Road	2254499
Hotel Mount Meridian	9-Robertson Road	2254946 / 2253204
Hotel Mount Pleasant	26/2, H.D. Lama Road	2254522
New Mount View Hotel	23 – M.N. Banerjee Lane	2252418
Hotel Nirvana	Dr S.K. Paul Road	2252909
Hotel North Star	11, H.D. Lama Road	2253938 / 2254499
		F: 2254499
Olive Dale Retreat	Gandhi Road	2252384
Palace Mahakal Hotel	9, Cooch Behar Road	2252026 / 2252056
The Parklane Hotel	N.C. Goenka Road	2256902 / 2254789
Hotel Penang	Ladenla Road	--
Pineridge Hotel	Chowrasta, The Mall	2254074 / 2253909
		F: 2253912
Hotel Plaza	41, Ladenla Road	2253883
		F: 2253883
Pradhan Hotel	Pradhan Niwas	2252103 / 2252718
	57, Gandhi Road	F: 2254330
Prestige Hotel	Ladenla Road	2253199 / 2252699
Hotel Priyanka	11/1, Toong Soong Road	2252160
Purnima Hotel	2/A, Cooch Behar Road	2253110
Pushpak Hotel	Chowrasta	2254497
Hotel Raj Palace	63/A, Ladenla Road	2254596
Hotel Raphkhog	6- N.B. Singh Road	2254632
Hotel Red Rose	37, Ladenla Road	2256062 / 2253895
		F: 2254390
Hotel Regent	2/1, H.D. Lama Road	2253109
Hotel Rockville	4, Rockville Road	2252513
Roma Holiday Inn	73/1, Gandhi Road	2254354 / 2256174
Sagarika Hotel	1, J.P. Sharma Road	2253090
Hotel New Samrat	63, Gandhi Road	2256444
Hotel Sangita	94, Dr Zakir Hussain Road	2252608
Hotel Savy	12, Gandhi Road	2254628
Seven Seventeen Hotel	H.D. Lama Road	2252017 / 2255099
		F: 2254717
Shambala Hotel	19, H.D. Lama Road	2252715 / 2252048
Hotel Shambhu	73, Gandhi Road	2254926, / 2253297
Shangrila Hotel	5, Nehru Road	2254149
Hotel Sherpa Intl.	5H, D.B. Giri Road	2252476

NAME	ADDRESS	PHONE / FAX
Hotel Shiker	72/A, Old Gandhi Road	2255141 / 2253490
Shrestha Lodge	15-Ladenla Road	2252961
Hotel Siddharth	9/1, T.N. Road, The Mall	2255364
Hotel Sinclairs	Gandhi Road	2256431-32 / 2256949 F: 2254355
Society Hotel	Robertson Road	2253315 / 2252316 F: 2252315
Hotel Springburn	70, Gandhi Road	2252054
Sterling Holiday Resort	Ghoom Monastery Road	2274365 / 2274215 F: 2274365
Hotel Sujata	12, Bilombre Road	22512152
Hotel Sunflower	Chowrasta, The Mall	2254391 / 2252052 F: 2254390
Hotel Sunrise	5, Dr Zaki Hussain Road	2253105
Hotel Swagat	Dr. Yen Singh Road	2255780
Hotel Swati	63, Ladenla Road	2252769
Hotel New Sweet Home	International, Gandhi Road	2256043
Hotel Swiss	M.G. Road	2256686 F: 2251396
Taj Hotel	Ladenla Road	2256374
Hotel Teesta	Hill Cart Road (New Bus Stand)	
Timber Lodge	Ladenla Road	
Tower View Hotel	8/1, Dr Zakir Hussain Road	2254452
Tribeni guest House	85/1, Dr Zakir Hussain Road	2253114
Hotel Tshering Denzongpa	6, J.P. Sharma Road	2254602
Hotel Valentino	6, Rock Ville Road	2252228
Three V. Lodge	9/A, Kutchery Road	2254311
Hotel West End	49, D.B. Giri Road	2255108
Windamere Hotel	Observatory Hill	2254041-42-44 F: 2254043 / 2254211
Hotel Yuma	5, Ladenla Road	2253943 / 2253986 F: 2253986
Hotel Zodiac	22/A/1, Gandhi Road	
Hotel Mohit	H.D.Lama Road	2254723 / 2254818 2253782 / 2255875 F: 2254351 / 2253782

HOTELS AND LODGES IN PELLING

NAME	LOCATION	PHONE
Bintam	Pelling	250682
Chinari	Pelling	258256
Garuda	Pelling	250614
Heaven	Pelling	258238
Hindusthan Lodge	Pelling	258247
Kabur	Pelling	258504
Kailash	Pelling	258257
Kecheperi	Pelling	250681
Ladakh Guest House	Pelling	--
Magnolia Lodge	Pelling	--
Mondal Lodge	Pelling	250684

NAME	LOCATION	PHONE
►► Namgay	Pelling	258269
►► Norbu Gang	Pelling	250566
►► Norbu Gang Resort	Pelling	258272
►► Panchok	Pelling	258237
►► Panorama	Pelling	258274
►► Parazong	Pelling	258239
►► Pelling	Pelling	258232
►► Pemachen	Pelling	250641
►► Phamrong	Pelling	250660
►► Pradhan	Pelling	250615
►► Resort Stellate	Pelling	250571
►► Samtenling	Pelling	258335
►► Sangha	Pelling	258322
►► Sarita	Pelling	250624
►► Seridana	Pelling	--
►► Sikkim Tourist Center	Pelling	250855
►► Silver Park	Pelling	258253
►► Simboo	Pelling	258246
►► Sinchur	Pelling	258288
►► Sister Guest House	Pelling	250569
►► Sitara	Pelling	258211
►► Snow White	Pelling	258246
►► Sonam Delek	Pelling	258286
►► Sun	Pelling	258207
►► Tashiling	Pelling	258287
►► Touristo	Pelling	258206
►► View Point	Pelling	258280
►► Window Park	Pelling	258212

INDEX

Notes

DISCOUNT COUPONS

20% OFF on food

Denzong Inn

Denzong Cinema Chowk, Gangtok

Denzong Inn offers the finest Chinese food in Gangtok

20% OFF on food

∾‖ HOTEL TASHI DELEK ‖∾

MG Marg, Gangtok

Enjoy Indian cuisine in Hotel Tashi Delek, a virtual landmark in Gangtok

Rs 600 OFF

Book through HEAT TRAVELS & TOURS
Siliguri, West Bengal

Rs 100 off per person for rafting on the Teesta (max 6 persons)

20% OFF on food

MG Marg, Gangtok

Pizzas and freshly-baked delicacies are the speciality at the Baker's Café

To entail the discount offered you need to present the book with the relevant coupon intact. Since this is a new concept, we suggest you do so at the onset, before ordering, just in case staff needs to confirm with the management.
The author and publisher are not responsible for any establishment reneging on their commitment of a discount. However, we would greatly appreciate your feedback on this discount offer and welcome suggestions to improve it.
Email us at: drivingholidays@yahoo.co.in

To entail the discount offered you need to present the book with the relevant coupon intact. Since this is a new concept, we suggest you do so at the onset, before ordering, just in case staff needs to confirm with the management.
The author and publisher are not responsible for any establishment reneging on their commitment of a discount. However, we would greatly appreciate your feedback on this discount offer and welcome suggestions to improve it.
Email us at: drivingholidays@yahoo.co.in

To entail the discount offered you need to present the book with the relevant coupon intact. Since this is a new concept, we suggest you do so at the onset, before ordering, just in case staff needs to confirm with the management.
The author and publisher are not responsible for any establishment reneging on their commitment of a discount. However, we would greatly appreciate your feedback on this discount offer and welcome suggestions to improve it.
Email us at: drivingholidays@yahoo.co.in

To entail the discount offered you need to present the book with the relevant coupon intact. Since this is a new concept, we suggest you do so at the onset, before ordering, just in case staff needs to confirm with the management.
The author and publisher are not responsible for any establishment reneging on their commitment of a discount. However, we would greatly appreciate your feedback on this discount offer and welcome suggestions to improve it.
Email us at: drivingholidays@yahoo.co.in

DISCOUNT COUPONS

20% OFF
on food

SHAMBHALA MOUNTAIN RESORT

Rumtek, Sikkim

Multi-cuisine dining and
a well stocked bar
await you at Rumtek

20% OFF
on food

Norbu Ghang Resort

Pellin, West Sikkim

While in Pelling, enjoy the
dining experience at
Norbu Ghang Resort

20% OFF
on food

taaja's ™
Creative Cusines

49 Laden Road, Darjeeling

Savour the
creative cuisine
of Taaja's

20% OFF
on food

Glenary's
The Master Baker

Nehru Road, Darjeeling

A trip to Darjeeling is
incomplete without
a visit to Glenary's

To entail the discount offered you need to present the book with the relevant coupon intact. Since this is a new concept, we suggest you do so at the onset, before ordering, just in case staff needs to confirm with the management.

The author and publisher are not responsible for any establishment reneging on their commitment of a discount. However, we would greatly appreciate your feedback on this discount offer and welcome suggestions to improve it.

Email us at: drivingholidays@yahoo.co.in

To entail the discount offered you need to present the book with the relevant coupon intact. Since this is a new concept, we suggest you do so at the onset, before ordering, just in case staff needs to confirm with the management.

The author and publisher are not responsible for any establishment reneging on their commitment of a discount. However, we would greatly appreciate your feedback on this discount offer and welcome suggestions to improve it.

Email us at: drivingholidays@yahoo.co.in

To entail the discount offered you need to present the book with the relevant coupon intact. Since this is a new concept, we suggest you do so at the onset, before ordering, just in case staff needs to confirm with the management.

The author and publisher are not responsible for any establishment reneging on their commitment of a discount. However, we would greatly appreciate your feedback on this discount offer and welcome suggestions to improve it.

Email us at: drivingholidays@yahoo.co.in

To entail the discount offered you need to present the book with the relevant coupon intact. Since this is a new concept, we suggest you do so at the onset, before ordering, just in case staff needs to confirm with the management.

The author and publisher are not responsible for any establishment reneging on their commitment of a discount. However, we would greatly appreciate your feedback on this discount offer and welcome suggestions to improve it.

Email us at: drivingholidays@yahoo.co.in

DISCOUNT COUPONS

20% OFF
on food

The Cindrella
HOTEL

Siliguri

To enjoy a vegetarian meal
drop in at
The Cindrella Hotel

20% OFF
on food

 Hotel Sai Kripa
private limited

Gangtok

The multi-cuisine
restaurant here provides
good quality meals

20% OFF
on food

The Royal Plaza

Gangtok

A lavish buffet spread
is served for breakfast,
dinner and lunch

20% OFF
on food

 Silver Oaks

Kalimpong

Old world candle lit dinners
at the Silver Restaurant
make a memorable evening

To entail the discount offered you need to present the book with the relevant coupon intact. Since this is a new concept, we suggest you do so at the onset, before ordering, just in case staff needs to confirm with the management.

The author and publisher are not responsible for any establishment reneging on their commitment of a discount. However, we would greatly appreciate your feedback on this discount offer and welcome suggestions to improve it.

Email us at: drivingholidays@yahoo.co.in

To entail the discount offered you need to present the book with the relevant coupon intact. Since this is a new concept, we suggest you do so at the onset, before ordering, just in case staff needs to confirm with the management.

The author and publisher are not responsible for any establishment reneging on their commitment of a discount. However, we would greatly appreciate your feedback on this discount offer and welcome suggestions to improve it.

Email us at: drivingholidays@yahoo.co.in

To entail the discount offered you need to present the book with the relevant coupon intact. Since this is a new concept, we suggest you do so at the onset, before ordering, just in case staff needs to confirm with the management.

The author and publisher are not responsible for any establishment reneging on their commitment of a discount. However, we would greatly appreciate your feedback on this discount offer and welcome suggestions to improve it.

Email us at: drivingholidays@yahoo.co.in

To entail the discount offered you need to present the book with the relevant coupon intact. Since this is a new concept, we suggest you do so at the onset, before ordering, just in case staff needs to confirm with the management.

The author and publisher are not responsible for any establishment reneging on their commitment of a discount. However, we would greatly appreciate your feedback on this discount offer and welcome suggestions to improve it.

Email us at: drivingholidays@yahoo.co.in

Discount Coupons

20% OFF
on food

The Chumbi Residency

Gangtok

An ideal place for a drink
and a relaxed meal

20% OFF
on food

 Nor Khill

Gangtok

This is the place
to enjoy traditional
Sikkimese cuisine

20% OFF
on food

 New Elgin

Darjeeling

Enjoy a leisurely tea
with cakes and pastries

20% OFF
on food

 **Elgin
Mt. Pandim**

Pelling

Stunning views makes
eating here a pleasurable
experience

To entail the discount offered you need to present the book with the relevant coupon intact. Since this is a new concept, we suggest you do so at the onset, before ordering, just in case staff needs to confirm with the management.
The author and publisher are not responsible for any establishment reneging on their commitment of a discount. However, we would greatly appreciate your feedback on this discount offer and welcome suggestions to improve it.
Email us at: drivingholidays@yahoo.co.in

To entail the discount offered you need to present the book with the relevant coupon intact. Since this is a new concept, we suggest you do so at the onset, before ordering, just in case staff needs to confirm with the management.
The author and publisher are not responsible for any establishment reneging on their commitment of a discount. However, we would greatly appreciate your feedback on this discount offer and welcome suggestions to improve it.
Email us at: drivingholidays@yahoo.co.in

To entail the discount offered you need to present the book with the relevant coupon intact. Since this is a new concept, we suggest you do so at the onset, before ordering, just in case staff needs to confirm with the management.
The author and publisher are not responsible for any establishment reneging on their commitment of a discount. However, we would greatly appreciate your feedback on this discount offer and welcome suggestions to improve it.
Email us at: drivingholidays@yahoo.co.in

To entail the discount offered you need to present the book with the relevant coupon intact. Since this is a new concept, we suggest you do so at the onset, before ordering, just in case staff needs to confirm with the management.
The author and publisher are not responsible for any establishment reneging on their commitment of a discount. However, we would greatly appreciate your feedback on this discount offer and welcome suggestions to improve it.
Email us at: drivingholidays@yahoo.co.in